Don't Make Me Go To School

Forward

A parent's view of how and why school refusal happens, the effects of school refusal, and why schools' attitudes to school refusers need to change. School refusal is a huge issue in post-Covid UK. For some young people, school's restrictive structures including teaching practices and uniforms are unsuitable from the start, and school refusal is only a matter of time. For others, a single event will trigger refusal, which could involve peer violence or be a matter, for example, of not being allowed to go to the toilet during a school day and subsequently developing a serious infection. Both scenarios happen routinely. Whether it's one or the other, or one of a myriad other hurdles young people have to navigate in their school days, the education system is increasingly unfit for purpose for many young people today.

What happened to Sam happens to thousands of teenagers in the UK, but remains hidden from sight because of fear of the repercussions that inevitably result from opening up and reaching out. Sam, like so many teenagers, was trapped within a school system that did not serve him well. But although Sam's school refusal felt like the end of the world at the time, Jenny is proud of her son who refused to go to school, and she wants the world to know that even though Sam was once one of many struggling teenagers, he reclaimed himself once the ordeal of school was over. She offers her story as a message of hope for parents who are floundering in the turmoil of school refusal. Her story is not meant as a diatribe against teachers, although the events she records here all happened when they should not have happened. There's good and bad in every profession, and there are also teachers struggling within the broken school system, though that's not the story Jenny is telling here. But if a young person rarely encounters the good, or encounters too much of the bad, they will inevitably suffer the consequences. The school system is creaking. Jenny wants to open up and diversify the national conversation about how we do schooling in the UK, and what we can, and must, do to save our young people from crisis.

At the time Sam's school refusal began, Jenny believed what the school told them, which can be summed up as: 'we don't have this problem with anyone else, Sam is the only one who struggles to get into school and we think your family must be dysfunctional otherwise it wouldn't be happening.' Sam and his family suffered unnecessarily from the conscious and unconscious bias that came with this untrue, unspoken yet keenly felt supposition. It wasn't

Sam who was dysfunctional, and it wasn't his parents. It was, and still is, the school system. Nowadays, there are more and more newspaper stories about teenagers who are not coping in schools that are increasingly unfit for purpose for many pupils. Their parents, once the initial shock of their child's school refusal has settled, can these days find support from online parent forums. That said, it is still likely to be a lonely path to tread. For Sam and his family, the journey was undoubtedly an isolating one because it was a long time until they realised that Sam was in actual fact a single drop in an invisible tsunami of school refusers, and the issue was set to get worse after the pandemic.

When you read Jenny's story, you might be shocked to find your own story written here. It is a sad fact that Sam's experience is replicated in up to a million homes the length and breadth of the UK. Sam could be your son or your daughter. His story will be familiar to many and identical to some. Sam is one in a million teenagers who have crashed out of school because of fear, anxiety or depression caused by school, not because of what the school system wanted him to believe: that he had innate problems and his family was failing to prioritise his academic success. School operates an inflexible system on an industrial scale, with thousands of pupils expected to behave in the same way (yet so much bad behaviour goes undetected or unchallenged), learn in the same way and look the same in their uniforms, even in the best schools. Alright for those who attend school, enjoy it and thrive, perhaps, but not for the many pupils who cannot cope within this kind of educational factory farming, and should not have to. These are the hidden and misunderstood many, the young people who become victims of the school system's failings. Jenny has had years to reflect on what happened to Sam and thousands upon thousands of other young people, so this book muses on her experiences. It reflects her point of view because when school refusal happens, parents are often left to guess why it's happening as the spiral into chaos happens in a fog. Their beloved young person cannot or will not say. With this in mind, Sam's story, and the story of how Jenny dealt with the collapse of family life as they knew it, begins here - as seen by Jenny rather than by Sam himself.

***

Sam lies in bed with his face to the wall, duvet pulled over his head, unmoving. It's Monday morning. Jenny has been trying to get him up for hours, and, now it's 9.30, an hour after the start of the school day, it's clear that her son is not going to make it into school. Again.

Again she will have to steel herself and call the unforgiving attendance office. Again she will have to say he has a tummy ache or a migraine. Again she will have to absorb the polite but frosty response, heavy with disapproval.

'Sam, what am I going to tell them this time?' She pleads.

No response. Nothing.

'Sam, can't you just get up and go in? Come on. Go in and we'll have a McDonald's later, after school.'

She's feeling the tension between helplessness and worry about what school will be thinking of them. She can feel her frustration rising.

Not even a stir.

It's been like this for weeks, no, months. It started with the occasional lesson he didn't, or couldn't, go to, then it turned into mornings off, then days of tummy aches, headaches and feeling too sick to go to school.

Every morning, Sam's friend dutifully knocked for him, waiting hopefully while he pretended to get ready. But more and more, Jenny had to let her know 'sorry, he's coming in a bit late today,' or 'sorry, he's not coming in today.' Sam's lovely friend never gave up. Eyes gleaming with honest love for Sam, she kept on calling for him against the odds, even when he wasn't managing to get up and keep up the pretense that he might go in.

'Hi Jenny, is Sam coming in today?'

'Hi Betty, I think he might be in later, thanks for calling, love.'

'Ah ok, bye then. Hope to see him later.' And off she'd go to catch the school bus.

And so it went on.

Eventually, Jenny had to suggest in the nicest possible way that Sam would most likely not be getting the bus in the morning any more so maybe Betty should stop calling.

'Ok,' said Betty gently, with an understanding smile. 'I hope he comes back to school soon. Say hi from me.'

Jenny can still see Betty walking away, forever as it happens, brown hair bouncing in the sunshine, off to school where she was flourishing, untouched by the troubles that were tormenting Sam. She was an academic girl who kept to herself. She was one of the lucky ones who school suited.

Jenny and Mike loved Betty for being such a steadfast friend to Sam and they missed her when she stopped calling. She had represented hope. It was good to know Sam had a steadfast friend like her, even if he did only see her on the bus in the whole of the school day. It still meant a lot to them. And for a while it felt like if Betty called there would be more of a chance of Sam going in. But only for a while, because, as it happened, it made no difference to Sam at all.

Slowly but surely Sam was giving clues to everyone that he couldn't manage school. But when you are in the thick of things it is not always possible to fully comprehend what's happening. Obviously something was wrong, but Jenny and Mike couldn't yet see what Sam was trying to tell them, and nor could anyone else. Sam's teachers barely mentioned his absences to begin with. Jenny wondered if they actually knew who Sam was or noticed when he was absent. If they did notice, they showed no sign of caring. Not one of them called to speak to Sam, Jenny or Mike to see how he was. There was obviously a problem, but the air was full of 'maybe try this and maybe try that' as well as a yet- to- be unidentified anxiety that hung in the air.

Most of us, unless home schooled, are brought up to expect certain societal rituals and milestones. Preschool leads to primary leads to secondary leads to college and then maybe university. That's just the way it is. Very few of us know about, or have experienced an alternative way of doing life. And if your child doesn't want to, or can't, go to school, what are you left with? What's the alternative? Most of us don't really know. Some of us might be suspicious of breaking from the norm and of those who do it. Home school is weird, right? At least it was before the pandemic. When children go to school, their parents can go to work; that's the way the system works. At school, parents assume their child is in a safe place, learning happily alongside their friends. They assume teachers notice what goes on in their classrooms and deal with poor behaviour when it happens. They assume their child is noticed and nurtured. But that assumption shattered for Jenny and Mike when Sam crashed out of school, and they were left questioning everything they had previously believed in. Initially, they had no idea what had happened to make Sam want to reject school or what was happening to him internally, and Sam himself was unable to explain. He just ceased to function and ceased to participate in life as they knew it.

Early on, when Jenny had insisted he 'try to get into school' he'd done it at first, for a few times, but then he struggled more and more until he just couldn't do it at all. She'd felt terrible trying to force the issue, as had Mike, but at the same time what alternative was there? She didn't know then what she knows now, and Sam's decline in attendance was gradual, if inexorable, so it took a while to fully dawn on them what was going on. Adding to the confusion was the fact that Sam said he said he wanted to go to school and he couldn't articulate why he wasn't able to go in, so it seemed right to encourage him to go.

Encouraging him to go in seemed the right thing to do for Sam, for the family and morally. They did not realise then what they know now: that many anxious school refusers say they want to go back to school because it's all they've ever known and they want the impossible: their old life back before it all went wrong. They assume school is all there is because it's all they've known, and without it, lying in bed on their own, they're staring into a terrifying void.

Many of the times she'd managed to coax Sam into the car and driven him to school, he'd been sick. Once in the school grounds when she'd tried to get him out of the car and into the school building. A number of times in the bushes on the drive there, so they'd had to turn around and drive home, Jenny's nerves in tatters. What was happening to Sam? What would she say to the school this time? What was she going to say to work about why she was so late? Jenny and Mike obviously knew what was happening to Sam was terribly wrong, but they were still under the impression they should try to get him into school and that a part of him still wanted to try, so this is what they did until the point of no return finally came, though the emotional and physical effects on Sam were becoming evident.

Early on, when Sam was still managing the occasional half day, school made appointments with the in-house counsellor. Sam saw the lady, a nicely presented person with kind eyes, a few times and he liked her. She was nice. She had honest intentions and a true desire to help young people. But it didn't work. Sam simply turned up for his counselling sessions, as long as they were in a separate building to where his peers were so that nobody could see him going in, then returned home unconvinced and unchanged.

After each session, the counsellor would emerge from her room with Sam and express the positive actions Sam had agreed to undertake.

'Sam says he will come into school tomorrow morning, just for IT and English, his favourite lessons,' she informed Jenny. 'That's great isn't it? A really great start, Sam, well done! Then, when you've done that, we can think about extending school time when you're ready, Sam, hey?'

Sam simply remained silent.

The following morning, Sam got up, put his uniform on and got in the car, throwing his backpack onto the back seat. Mike and Sam set off on the three mile drive to school and Jenny went to work with a black hole in her stomach as she always did when she had to leave Sam to his struggle.

Calling Mike to see how it had gone, she found out the inevitable.

'He made me stop, said Mike, unhappily. 'Then he got out and sat by the side of the road shaking. He just couldn't do it, and I can't do this to him anymore, Jen. We need to do something else. This isn't working.'

It became clear that Sam was telling the counsellor what she wanted to hear; agreeing to give school a try then not being able to attend when the time actually came. This happened time and again. It was, and remains obvious to Jenny that a child can be persuaded to say 'yes, it's not so bad, I'll go into school tomorrow' when it's not actually tomorrow yet. They'll have the best of intentions and will say anything to make the adult they're talking to happy so they can get out of there and not have to think about the problem anymore. But when tomorrow comes, going to school becomes impossible again. Children's emotional response to situations is always more immediate and powerful than their rational response, whether or not they are able to mask it with the behaviours of acquiescence drummed into them by school or wider society. It's the same for everyone. Human nature. Sam had learned to say yes, probably even meaning it at the time because he was desperate for things to be normal, but self preservation and terror of school meant he would never be able to go in. He couldn't fight so flight was his only option.

Eventually, school informed Jenny that a meeting would be necessary to sort out the problem of Sam's non- attendance, so she left work early on the assigned day to meet the deputy head, Mrs Jones. Dread formed in the pit of Jenny's stomach as she made the drive from her workplace to the school. If she, a grown woman who is free to leave school whenever she wishes, felt like this, goodness knows how Sam, a teen who was trapped in the place from morning to mid afternoon felt. Jenny thought she herself might be sick as she made her way up the steps to the school's entrance and into the reception area. At least the receptionist was friendly, but the fear of being judged by the deputy head fizzed within her. Worse still was the fear that her son was being judged for his inability to attend school. This was the atmosphere she had been picking up from the communications with the school attendance office. 'Follow me,' said the receptionist, kindly, 'Mrs Jones is expecting you in her room upstairs.' Jenny had then followed her through the dismal, grey echoing corridors, enlivened, at least, by displays of pupils' work.

Though superficially smiling and polite, Mrs Jones, the deputy, was made of steel. Her job was to insist on good attendance and 'maintain school standards' and she was not going to make any bones about it. 'We can give Sam a reduced timetable for the time being,' she had said. 'But we will be expecting him to increase attendance as time goes on. Failing that, we will be looking at making a no names consultation with MASH and considering fines if his attendance does not improve.'

Jenny could only stare in disbelief as the shock of Mrs Jones's perfunctory solutions sank in, as if in saying them the problem would simply melt away. When she finally summoned the courage to respond, her voice was shaking. 'Are you seriously telling me that your answer to Sam's crisis is to fine us? Are you actually serious?' She had spluttered, incredulously. Still naive about the school system, she was not prepared for Mrs Jones's blunt words.

'Sam does not have a mental health diagnosis so we have no option but to treat him as a school refuser who is failing to meet the required standards of behaviour and attendance.' Mrs Jones had continued. 'Unless there is a diagnosis and therefore a good reason for him to be missing school, he is in effect truanting, and you have a duty to make sure he attends.'

Jenny had struggled to resist the urge to do or say something she might later regret. Leaning forward in her seat and fixing Mrs Jones with an incredulous stare, she could feel her eyes stinging with tears of anger and despair.

'So my son is violently sick every day at the thought of having to attend your school, he's scared and lonely, he's lost all his friends, and we are a family in crisis… and you sit there with no humility or self reflection at all and threaten me with fines? Is this a joke?' She was not going to hold back now. She couldn't. 'What do you think we are doing every morning, Mrs Jones? Lying in bed snoring without a care in the world? We've been trying everything possible to help Sam get into school. Have you? I for one haven't heard from a single one of Sam's teachers. Does anyone care about him and actually want to help him? Or are you happy just to dole out fines?'

At that moment she realised what Sam was up against: a system that does not understand the complexity of school anxiety and the devastation it wreaks on families; a system geared to achieve a 95% or above attendance record to achieve a 'good' rating from Ofsted which, it seemed to Jenny, matters to schools over and above everything else, including proper provision and care for struggling pupils.

Jenny's first meeting with Mrs Jones gave her a wake up call and shocked her deeply. She hadn't known what to expect, but she had thought there might be some kind words passed on from Sam's teachers or some work given to him to keep him in the loop and make him feel like he was at least thought about. None of this happened. Instead she was threatened with fines in an atmosphere thick with accusation, and Sam was treated as a defiant truant because he had no mental health diagnosis. How was he supposed to get a diagnosis before his school refusal happened? It seemed absurd to her that the evidence in front of them now was disregarded because nobody had foreseen the future.

Jenny sighs and turns to leave the room, looking back in anguish at the shape under the duvet that is her 15 year old son. She is overwhelmed by the depths of Sam's despair. What can it feel like to lie in bed for hours and hours and hours? Nothing to get up for, nobody to speak to. Completely locked in. Every day she tries so hard to enthuse him. Would he like to go for a walk? How about a haircut? Fancy getting a McDonald's? But every day Sam lies there facing the wall, all hope of a recovery from whatever terrible malaise has gripped him fading from view. When she shuts his bedroom door behind her, the overwhelming sense of sadness she has known for many many months sweeps over her and she is exhausted. She slumps against the closed door and slides to the floor until, knees bent and backside on the floor, she convulses with sobs. A mother shattered by what is happening to her precious and beloved boy. Tears flow and exhaustion infuses every limb. Once a high-functioning professional with a smooth running, happy family, she is now an emotionally frazzled woman on the verge of a nervous breakdown. She gives in to exhaustion and allows herself to sob impotent tears of grief for the son she wants so much to be happy and for the life they have lost.

An hour or so later, she pulls herself together because, as with every day, she has to. She wipes her eyes and drags herself to her feet. She needs a coffee; strong and black. She is all too aware that Sam will have heard her outburst and she feels ashamed of herself.

'Love you,' she whispers to her son who lies under the covers behind the shut door, then, running her fingers gently down the door as if she might be stroking Sam's cheek, she takes herself off to assemble the fragmented pieces of her sanity in the kitchen with her coffee.

Jenny Googles MASH and finds it's a multi agency government organisation that provides 'no names consultations' and advice to schools - a new world to her. She learns that the people who operate MASH are trained in safeguarding and they consider children who are not in school to be 'at risk'. At risk, she learns, of 'failing to get an education' or of physical or emotional abuse, presumably from people at home or possibly at the hands of gangs or extremists. The more Jenny reads, the more it dawns on her that these safeguarders, though they have children's best interests at heart, do not posses the depth of understanding of the complexity that lies behind the 'failure to attend school' for school phobia. In black and white terms, they believe all children who are not at school are 'at risk.' They do not seem to understand that non attendance does not equate to abuse, and seem never to have heard of school anxiety so sure are they that school is the right and proper place for all children to be. Of course if a child is at risk of any kind of abuse or harm there should be people working on their behalf who are able to act quickly to prevent it, and Jenny understands the key role schools play in protecting children from multiple harms. But school refusal does not equate to abuse. How could the system allow abuse and non-attendance to be lumped together so clumsily so as to potentially cause criminalisation of caring, loving parents who are trying their best for their child? And how and why should a loving family like her own be threatened with fines and MASH? Later, after more research, Jenny understood such issues arise because schools conflate the various problems that lead to poor attendance. Failure to attend school alerts schools to children missing out on their human right to get an education, and their reaction is usually draconian and undifferentiated, failing to filter the reasons behind non attendance and so treating the anxious pupil the same as the child off school for a two week skiing holiday or the child off school because of a harm taking place. The threat of fines for parents who don't or can't get their child into school to access their 'right to an education' is held over them like the sword of Damocles as if there can be no excuses at all for non attendance, even if the act of going to school is detrimental to the mental health of the young person - something educationalists won't accept. And besides, thinks Jenny, education is more than sitting in a classroom being instructed on any given subject, education is about learning how to be in the world and how to find your own unique place in it. So what about when your unique place in the world is negated?

This is a later thought process, however. At the time, Jenny was too shocked by her own circumstances to piece together where Sam fitted into the national picture. She reeled from what she had read, shocked by the irony. It was becoming more and more apparent to her that by refusing to go into school, Sam was safeguarding himself from a dysfunctional school system that was not serving him well, though he was not able to articulate why. This multi agency safeguarding team, however, would see it differently - if Mrs Jones called them. They'd say they are concerned that Sam is 'at risk' of failing to get an education and she and Mike are 'failing' to ensure he gets into school so he can achieve his potential. But, Jenny questioned, did they really want equality of education for Sam? Or was it really compliance they are after? How many of them really cared if Sam achieved his potential or not? If they did, surely they'd be sending work home for him to do and calling home to see how he was, but there was none of that. Nobody at school was behaving as though they cared about Sam's education. In reality, thought Jenny, isn't it that they don't like people who challenge the system or their authority, so they are incapable of recognising the inappropriateness of fines when the challenge to their authority comes in the form of school phobia? Under their system, there is no difference between fining parents for taking a child out of school to go on holiday, and fining the parents of a suicidal, school phobic child as far as she could see. How, thought Jenny, could this be right?

What, for goodness sake, is the worst that could happen if Sam didn't get any GCSEs? On the other hand, if he was forced into school (not that this would actually be possible any more) and became more and more depressed, goodness knows what the outcome might be. Sam had spent many hours hiding in the school toilets rather than attend lessons that for one reason or another he could not cope with. None of the teachers contacted her to let her know he wasn't present in class. Either they didn't know he was missing or they didn't care. The only reason she knew he spent his time in the loos was because he constantly texted her asking her to come and get him because he was ill. Was that a safe situation for Sam to be in? Jenny didn't feel it was. Why would she send him to a place where he was uncared for and felt unsafe, if 'sending him' was still an option, which it wasn't? And how dare the people operating this dysfunctional system presume to lecture her on safeguarding when school itself was the unsafe place? Safeguard the vulnerable children who need it, but don't persecute parents for trying to save their child from a mental health catastrophe!

Reeling from the awful realisations of the day, Jenny felt sick to the stomach at the trap that had been laid for them. The assumption that something must be amiss within the family, or that a child is being somehow wilful if they are not attending school shocked her. With eyes and minds blinkered to the possibility that the school system might be unmanageable for some children, and that many children are being failed by school, this was not a system Jenny wanted Sam to have anything to do with any more, and she certainly had no intention of continuing to try to force him back there.

Jenny shuddered with fear when it dawned on her the family would come under suspicion of some kind of wrong doing. If Mrs Jones put the wheels in motion, teachers and other safeguarders would be prying into their family life and viewing them through a stained lens. She and Mike would be tried and found wanting and they would be punished, most probably with fines for non attendance which they couldn't afford and which is a completely inappropriate response to school phobia. Sam would then suffer under the pressure and tension resulting from all of this, and his little brother would suffer the knock on consequences too. As the awfulness of their situation opened up before her, any faith she had once had in the school system evaporated and all her trust in it shrivelled to dust.

As time went on and Sam fell further and further out of the system, Jenny was made to feel Sam was the only pupil ever to suffer anxiety about going to school, and this contributed to, and enabled, the feeling of suspicion that what was happening to Sam was the fault of his family: a failure in parenting. This made Jenny shrink inside and feel ashamed about seeking help, not that she knew who to turn to or where she would go to find help. It was as if they were contaminated. Losers who couldn't deal with the way things should be. She felt school was pointing the finger at them and school staff were rolling their eyes about them behind their backs. There was no sense of humility from school, and no sense that anyone genuinely cared about Sam. No work was sent home for Sam to get on with, no teachers called to see how he was getting on, and Sam was left with the feeling he had simply been erased from his year group, as if he had never existed. How could it be that on the one hand 'education is a human right and every child must attend school' yet on the other hand not a single scrap of work was sent to Sam when it really mattered? If school cared so much about safeguarding Sam's education, why didn't they ensure he received work and encouraging words from his teachers? Jenny had asked them often enough. Through the confusion and sadness, Jenny was beginning to see that they were not prepared to help, educate or even be kind unless Sam conformed.

Hours drift by and Jenny knows Sam will not get up. He will lie in bed all day again just like he has on all the other long, dark days preceding today. The strain of knowing her son is using his precious time on earth lying in bed alone day in day out bores into her brain. The pain, both emotional and now physical (headaches, tight muscles, stomach aches) as a result of the anguish is intolerable. She has tried to engage him in activities he used to enjoy: swimming, dog walks, visits to friends, but most of the time he cannot be persuaded. He pulls his duvet over his head and turns to face the wall, unreachable. But she will never give up on him. Every so often he might accompany her somewhere or go to hang out with a friend who lives down the road, but this is rare. When it does happen it is like Christmas has come and Santa has delivered the best present imaginable. There is an unspoken but tangible family fanfare and, communicating telepathically, everyone rallies round to try to make it last. Sam is engaged in conversation, encouraged to play a board game, invited to watch a film, asked to choose his favourite meal. Jenny, Mike and Sam's little brother do everything humanly possible to encourage him to stay with them, to live a little, to find a place in the world.
She will try again today.

After her awakening to the school system, Jenny feels angry. Sometimes she feels so angry she could explode because she is so indignant on behalf of Sam, and the discrepancy between what actually goes on in their household and what the powers that be seem to think happens. They haven't the faintest clue about how hard they have tried. Her hands tremble and she can feel her face flush red at the injustice of the situation. She's not going to be bullied by Mrs Jones and her threats. How dare she refer her precious, loving family to MASH? How dare they negate Sam's pain and their family struggle? How can they fail to see that normality has ended for them and they are all trying their best to deal with a terrible situation? How can school not realise that their friendships, routines and ability to work are all crumbling around their ears as they try to deal with the terrible unfathomable thing that is happening to their son? Answering her own questions, it's because they think they know what's best for Sam, whilst simultaneously having no lived experience to enlighten them from their prejudices. So convinced and invested are they that they are incapable of seeing a different perspective. Products of an education system that worked for them, they feel it should work for everyone, and if it doesn't, it's the fault of the individual who is struggling. They call it 'failing.' How dare Mrs Jones not look to her school and its competitive, restrictive, divisive systems that can't offer a decent education to a pupil who needs a different approach and can only resort to threats of fines for non compliance? With her increasing awareness, Jenny found her courage and determined to stand up to Sam's school. There was nothing wrong with Sam that wasn't of the system's making and she would not let them get away with punishing him for their own failings. How dare they?

In the early months of Sam's school refusal, Mrs Jones encouraged Jenny to believe Sam was the only one of his peer group who was unable to go to school, and because she didn't yet have the wider national picture, Jenny believed hers to be only family to be living through this nightmare. Weren't the parents of his childhood friends posting endless social media updates about the parties, the accomplishments, the academic successes achieved by their children with what felt like cruel frequency? Proof that life for Sam's peers was perfect. Freshly coiffed boys in groups grinned at her from social media photos, making her feel wretched and excluded.
'Look at the fish Billy caught today'!'
'Cool haircut, Toby.'
'Happy 15th, Adam. Love you loads.'
And so on and so on. Endless success stories of the kids who fit the mould and made the grade. There

they all were, out and about living life to the full while Sam lay in bed upstairs on his own.

Jenny hated them. People who used to be her friends, she detested. Her eyes stung with tears when she looked at the endless photos of success stories and happiness. It was as if they were spiting her, spiting Sam, and spiting their whole past and present. She wishes she could be the better person and write that she was happy for them, but all she felt was crushing pain because Sam was hidden away and was clearly not doing well like they were. She hated their smug, public showing off.

The truth is, of course, that they were indifferent, and that was immeasurably worse. All these people who had spent hours at her house with their son or daughter, drinking coffee, playing, sharing lunch, watching films, staying for sleepovers, all the usual things friends do with each other in those years of bringing up pre teen children, were now absent from their lives without a backward glance. Sam had been erased from the social picture and now spent his days alone in bed. Not one friend besides Betty in the early days of Sam's school refusal, and occasionally his mate down the road, called to see how he was or hang out. And only one or two of her own friends had asked how Sam was doing. It was as if Sam had become a dirty secret. Sam's erasure, which had been creeping up over the weeks and months, was now complete, and Jenny found herself hating all these ex friends with their apparently callous indifference.

Jenny is now, again, convulsing with sobs. They roar from her with unstoppable force, received by a silent house. The injustice of what is happening to her boy, and to them as a family, is too much to bear and momentarily she wants her life to end, because in so many ways it has already ended. She has tried so hard to make things better yet the hurdles are raised higher around every turn. Life feels intolerable and yet she must continue. What alternative is there? Though buried within his own lockdown, Sam needs her and her love for him outweighs her despair. The gut wrenching knowledge that she must eventually get up, dust herself down, get her work done, make lunch for Sam and deliver it to his room in the hope he will eat something and try to establish some sense of normalcy forms a kernel of determination in her gut. She will do these things today, she will do these things again tomorrow and she will continue to do these things for as long as it takes no matter how it ends. Every parent who loves their kid knows this is the way it must be, even when hope is fading from view.

Early life for Sam had been wonderful. A happy infant, Jenny and Mike provided a stable home for him, plenty of love and encouragement for anything he showed an interest in. He was read to, they watched films together, they had fun family holidays and had lots of friends. In fact, Sam was the go-to playmate in his class from nursery through pre-school and in the early primary years. He was imaginative and fun, he loved adventure games with toy guns and costumes, and his friends always wanted to come to his house to play with him. They'd run around the house and garden playing all kinds of fantasy Sci Fi role play games and the place was always full of fun and laughter.

One of his special friends was Anna. She was wild and loved Sam. They were inseparable, doing everything together inside and out of school. For four years this bond appeared to be unshakeable, but towards the end of Year 4 things started to change, and the main cause of this change was, it seemed to Jenny and Mike, football.

When Sam was in the later years of primary school, around Year 4, Jenny and Mike had done what many parents in the village and wider community do: encourage their child to participate in local football events. Dutifully, they would take Sam to the matches on Saturday morning, chat with the other parents and cheer Sam and his friends on as they played. But although they had an inkling that Sam was not really that keen on football, they didn't spot the more corrosive aspect of what was going on within the group of friends until the damage had already been done. Sam's lack of commitment to the sport was being logged in the children's minds. Every missed goal or half baked tackle was met with derision, sometimes verbalised, sometimes simply conveyed in an expression. The only male heroes were football heroes and every boy except Sam wanted to be one. His friends didn't pick him to be on their team because he didn't have the drive and commitment. He became the one left over after picking sides who one team had to tolerate being on their side or cast as a sub. It started happening every day at school, though the overall change in attitude shifted over time. It wasn't that Sam's friends were always outright horrible or hostile, but their attitude to him nonetheless changed and there was distance where relationships had previously been tight, and this was confusing for Sam. He picked up the atmosphere without fully understanding why it was happening, perhaps because some of his friends still occasionally conceded and played the games they used to play before football became the all-consuming obsession. As the boys got older, football became more serious and the measure by which they judged each other. It wasn't enough to enjoy kicking a ball around now; you had to walk the walk and talk the talk. Sam didn't have a passion for the game but was happy to kick a ball around. His lack of competitive spirit didn't cut the mustard with the other players, however; they wanted to win. They formed their collective identity through football.

'Do you want to come back after?' Sam asked his friends as he always used to after an event or after school. Previously, his invitation had been met with excited agreement, but in the later months of Year 4 his invitations were met with 'I've got a match on' instead of eager acceptance. Anna no longer wanted to play with him either, preferring to play football with the in-crowd.

There came a day when Sam no longer wanted to play football. His reputation as a sub was beginning to take hold in the children's minds and he felt it himself because he just wasn't interested in the game. Instead of going to the field on Saturday mornings he stayed at home and listened to the children's shouts and yells from the pitch echoing around the village whilst playing by himself or with his brother at home. Sometimes, Sam, his little brother, Jenny and Mike would go on bike rides, play with Lego or go swimming instead of playing football, and things would be fine at home. But at school others were forming a collective identity as football players and Sam was not part of it. Whatever he was interested in didn't count for anything because football was all that mattered. This prevailing attitude was echoed in the wider village community where the 'football parents' considered there was something not quite right about you if you weren't into football.

As the children moved up to Year 5 and identities started to take shape, Sam would suffer minor slights and put downs. Then Anna, his best friend, deserted him for the class football hero and his outsider status was cemented. It wasn't that he was overtly bullied, so it seemed to Jen and Mike, it was more that his interests simply did not align with the majority and claimed no validation. So Sam went from being a confident, happy little boy to a nervous, unsure young adolescent. As stated, it didn't strike them that Sam was being bullied, it was more that his hobbies and interests no longer aligned with those of his classmates. He was annoyed that all his friends wanted to play football and sad that they no longer wanted to do the things he enjoyed doing. This would have been fine if there was some give and take, but it wasn't like that in Sam's particular class - football was everything. It was unlucky for Sam that every other boy in his class was obsessed with football while he really couldn't care less, and this difference in attitude set him apart with no one to share his interests. It was sad for Jenny and Mike to see him trying to 'keep in' with the boys who rated him poorly because of his lack of football prowess. In another class with different boys (it was the boys who dominated this particular class) there might have been someone who shared his interests, but Sam was on his own here.

When Jenny looks back, she marvels at how so much of this attitude and behaviour went unspoken and not fully realised at the time, but how clear as daylight it all is now. She realises that, in the confusion of shifting friendships and loyalties, she and Mike had gone into coping mode, making up for the disappointments and social slights by providing other opportunities for Sam whenever they could. And yet throughout this time damage was being done and Sam's confidence and development were being eroded. His sense of self was being diminished because in his class no skills were valued or celebrated other than football skills and the teachers were not interested in challenging the norm. If only Jenny and Mike could have seen clearly then what was happening to Sam, they could have taken action. They could have moved house or moved him to a different primary school where there might have been a differently oriented cohort. Yet somehow everything was slippery and unclear. They were living uncertainly, feeling things weren't quite right without fully understanding how or why, though the football issue was obvious. Sometimes a friend would come to play and, relieved, they'd think maybe things were alright after all. Another time Sam might gain an achievement sticker for school work and they'd wonder if they had been imagining Sam's social discomfort at school. But positive events were few and far between and they seized them too gratefully when they came. Confusion was the prevailing mood of Year 4.

Jenny does not view childhood through rose coloured spectacles, she knows that childhood friendships ebb and flow and she understands issues will arise in a child's formative years. That's just an inevitable part of growing up and children benefit from learning resilience to help them deal with life's ups and downs. But when systems are restrictive, friendships restrained by the formation of 'friendship groups' which are governed by often brutal unspoken forces are embedded into a child relentlessly from a young age, damage will inevitably be done. Resilience then becomes an unfair expectation because the child is up against impossible odds.

Sam's situation was not helped by the primary school. In fact, at times Jenny believes it was caused by the school. The head teacher toadied to the village big cheeses and one or two of the teachers she employed were partisan and unkind. Unfortunately for Sam, the Year 4 teacher, Mrs Smith, was one of these. Colluding with the in crowd, she would routinely humiliate Sam, making him sit at the front at her desk because he wasn't one of the football kids who all wanted to sit together, eager to have a fall guy to pick on as groups of kids often do to ensure their own status is upheld.

Jenny recalls phoning Mrs Smith to take her to task about her treatment of Sam. A child in the class had a visitor from Germany staying with him, which meant, for a reason only known to Mrs Smith, that the German child was to sit in Sam's place and Sam would therefore be seated at her desk at the front so that the child and his German friend could sit together. No consultation, no consideration of the effect on Sam. Jenny had tried to be polite.

'Sam said he has to sit at the front of the class at your table to make way for a visitor,' she'd said to Mrs Smith over the phone the morning after she had found out what had happened. 'He feels sad at being separated from the others and self-conscious at having attention drawn to him by having to sit at your desk. Please can he be allowed to sit in his usual place today?'

'I haven't got time for this,' Mrs Smith had barked at her before slamming the receiver down. This was her response to a polite request to consider a young person she was employed to nurture: apparently self-absorbed fury at having her authority questioned. Shaking, Jenny had tried calling back but Mrs Smith was too busy to speak to her. Jenny phoned the head and insisted on calling a meeting to complain about Mrs Smith's behaviour, exasperated at having to deal with a so-called professional who behaved like an aged toddler.

There had been a meeting, but Jenny had been made to feel like the one who was at fault. Sam was deemed 'sensitive', so Mrs Smith's behaviour could not be questioned. Nobody would address the issue of a member of staff slamming the phone down on a parent. Instead of using their power to help Sam, Mrs Smith in particular, but also the primary school head, used it to reduce him further by making both Sam and Jenny feel like an annoyance.

Sam started refusing to go to school so there was another meeting, again with the emphasis on Sam being 'the issue', followed by a plan for Mrs Smith to greet him at the car in the mornings and take him into school. At the time, Jenny and Mike had been grateful, thinking she was now genuinely trying to be helpful. So when Mrs Smith dragged Sam from the car into school and they were told 'he was fine when you'd gone' they felt relieved. Some days were easier than others, but at least he was going in and life could go on.

What they didn't know until later was that Sam was sat on his own in class and left on his own when the others went off to play football at break times, his isolation deepening, his world shrinking, his fear of failure and rejection growing and the seed of depression beginning to take shoot. He had different interests to the other boys in his class but his interests were not valued, so Sam was being invalidated and his confidence was in tatters, though Jenny and Mike had not realised then how unconfident, tense and anxious he was becoming.

Year 6 was better. This was because the teacher was excellent. She saw Sam's strengths and wasn't interested in pleasing the hierarchy of parents. Her interests genuinely lay with the children and she recognised and dealt with any troublesome dynamics. Her strength and kindness had an influence on the class as a whole, and while Sam did not regain the status of his early years, seemed to be happy enough to go into school.

Sam remembers his Year 6 teacher as someone who cared about everyone, not just the few, and as someone who made him feel valued and wanted. This is the mark of a great teacher. It's easy to feel valued if you are part of the established mainstream. Far less so if your interests lay elsewhere. She valued everyone no matter what, and normalised rather than accentuated differences. Jenny feels grateful that Sam has at least one enduring memory of having felt cared for and valued at his primary school - he still talks about this teacher fondly. Everyone knows a kind teacher can make the world of difference in a child's life. But a teacher can only do so much when the odds are stacked against you and school systems are inflexible and harmful.

All schools have landmark events and the Cycling Proficiency Test is one of them. Cycling proficiency takes place in Year 6 in Sam's village primary school.

All the kids in the year group take part and passing the test is a big deal to every one of them. Parents of children who have been through it will understand how much passing the test matters to children in Year 6, just check out any parenting forum to understand what a big deal it is. But most parents believe it might be fun and possibly useful to gain your cycling proficiency badge, but it is an indicator of nothing and will have no lasting impact on your cycling ability whether you pass or fail. To a primary pupil, however, it's a landmark test and success is of utmost importance - a view encouraged by their teachers who believe in tests.

What parents might not realise, Mike and Jenny included at the time, is that cycling proficiency examiners are obliged to fail two pupils in every group because they are not allowed a hundred percent pass rate. The reasoning behind this is not only illogical but also potentially catastrophic for the fledgling individuals who are chosen to fail. This is because the chances are it is likely to be the same children who fail at cycling proficiency as who fail at other things in school, and the accumulation of failures inevitably leads to low self esteem.

On the morning of the cycling proficiency test, Sam set out with his classmates in their cycle helmets and high viz jackets. Smiling as they ushered the earnest, concentrating children through the streets, the facilitators waved at parents who watched the line of wobbling young cyclists from the sidelines. Sam had set off alongside the others, doing his best and focusing well. He was just as good as any of them. 'Try your best but don't worry,' Jenny and Mike had told him. But at the end of the test the examiner gathered the children around her and announced to everyone that they had passed - except for Sam and another boy who, she said, failed. It was because he had put his foot down to steady himself at one point along the way, just as some of the others had done but more prolonged, apparently. Needless to say, Sam was devastated. Which child wouldn't be when singled out for failure so randomly and publicly? Sam couldn't understand why putting his foot down would result in a fail for him but not for anyone else. The failure must, therefore, really be to do with Sam himself, he reasoned. The examiner didn't like him, maybe. Or was it because he was just useless at everything? Useless at football, useless at cycling, useless at everything other people valued. There was no need for Sam or indeed any child to have failed the test. Instead, all children doing the course could have been rewarded with a certificate of participation. Why not? What difference would it make? Jenny has heard arguments for the test to drive home a message about competition and striving. But Jenny believes to argue such a thing about an irrelevant test is pointless and damaging, because there are no sensible grounds for failure.

The only message given to Sam that day was if he participated in tests he would fail and be humiliated because so far this was what he had known. Failure struck Sam very hard indeed because it was becoming part of his identity. It could so easily have been different if things were more thoughtfully organised, but school systems punish people like Sam and turn them into 'failures'. A reorganisation of approaches and educational attitudes could do so much to help young people who always find themselves at the failing end when there is no good reason to fail them.

There comes a turning point in a child's life when they realise that mum and dad can't make the bad things that happen to them in the outside world better, and for Sam this point had come. They tried telling him they themselves had never taken a cycling proficiency test and they had just careered around on their bikes anyway. But it was no good. This was Sam's life and Sam's reality, and he had experienced another public failure. He was learning, though he never articulated it, that other people, including his peers and teachers, thought he wasn't good enough. The loss of status and public failures in competitive fields that had been imposed on him were now forming his identity and he must have felt powerless to do anything about it.

Towards the end of Year 6, the children went to an Outdoor Education Centre by way of a final school trip as a year group. It was a residential trip, and, like his classmates, Sam wanted to share a room with his friends. The class was asked to put the names of two friends they would like to share with on a piece of paper and hand it to the teacher. Jenny had learned to dread anything like this because Sam always seemed to lose out. The odds were stacked against him, especially as Mrs Smith was involved in running the trip.

Sure enough, when Sam returned home from school the next day he told her he had been put in the 'leftovers group', as Mrs Smith put it. Jenny had once again tried to get in touch with school to see if anything could be done, but no. 'Nobody wanted to share with Sam,' she was told, bluntly.

She had cried then too. The unkindness of the teacher had had such a profound effect on their family. A kind word here, a little boost there could have helped him; that's all it would have taken. His peers liked him and would not have minded sharing a room with him. They might not have chosen him over the boys they played football with but it didn't mean they disliked him. One or two of them might have passed comment if they hadn't been put with all their chosen friends, but a thoughtful teacher could have managed the situation and made sure everyone was happy. Instead, Sam was informed nobody wanted to share with him and left to deal with that information on his own. It wasn't that anyone would object to sharing with him, it's just that the system of choosing was set up to make it look that way to an ill-informed and unimaginative teacher. It was as if Mrs Smith was doing it on purpose and enjoying the emotional pain it caused him. Sam did go on the trip to his credit, but Jenny is not sure how much he enjoyed it because he didn't say much about it when he returned. Mrs Smith's unkindness remains indelibly etched into Sam's memory to this day. She had the power to do good, but her lack of imagination and her unkindness meant she caused immeasurable harm. Unfortunately, this humiliation in the hands of the school was not Sam's last. Perhaps the most hurtful blow of all was dealt in the Year 6 leavers assembly. Mike was at work, but Jenny had taken time off to be there for Sam's big last event. Parents were gathered in groups reminiscing, many in tears because their child was leaving the safe space of primary school to start the next phase of their school career. Not Jenny. She longed for a fresh start for Sam and all the promise that would bring. She couldn't wait for Sam to leave!

The children had stood on stage in the hall and there had been drama sketches, songs and speeches. Although Jenny could have predicted the school trip situation, nothing could have prepared her for this. There she sat, smiling with the affection of one who looks back over the years and finds fond memories, as one by one the children received certificates from the head teacher for one thing or another: best footballer, most progress made, kindest in the class etc... 'I wonder what they'll say about Sam,' she thought to herself as the certificates rolled out and children received them proudly and made their way off the stage in a little procession. But then, suddenly, the certificates stopped rolling out and that was the end. Sam was one of three children who had not received a certificate. Had they paused? Had they forgotten him? In her confusion, she realised the head teacher was giving a summing up speech and it dawned on her no. Sam had not, and would not, receive an award. There was simply nothing good enough about her son to warrant an end of year award.

They could find nothing good to say about him and they couldn't even be bothered to make something up. Jenny stared at Sam in anguish, unable to comprehend how people in charge of children's development could be so negligent, but she couldn't work out whether or not he had noticed. Then, aghast, she realised he was so used to being sidelined or left out he hadn't even registered this final humiliation. Either that, or he had simply come to expect it. Jenny was so shocked her entire being shook with a combination of tension, rage and sadness. The groups of parents, the smiling faces, the tears and hugs, the biscuits and coffee passed her by in a blur as she summoned all her courage to stay the distance when all she wanted to do is grab Sam by the hand and run. Her sense of isolation deepened when she realised no one else had noticed what had happened to Sam because they were so full of pride for their own child, and if she'd tried to say anything she would likely be accused of being a killjoy. Thus the school had succeeded in emotionally harming a child and isolating his family. Thank goodness Sam was leaving. It couldn't happen soon enough.

Sam's primary school and this peer group had set the stage for Sam's school career. Only it was still too early for Jenny to see it. Instead, she clung to the hope that secondary school would be better for him once he had left the primary school behind. There would be a healthier mix of people, kinder teachers and more interesting subjects to study. He would surely flourish once he moved on up. And primary school had not been all bad. When she looked back, Jenny could remember lots of good times despite the pervasive lack of inclusivity that undoubtedly formed part of the school's identity. But much sadness lies in the knowledge that with a few tweaks in attitudes and procedures, some harms could have been easily and effortlessly prevented.

Two years after Sam left, the village primary school was put into 'special measures' by Ofsted. When Jenny was told of the impending inspection she predicted the outcome correctly. She knew from personal experience that elements of Sam's primary school were harmful to a particular cohort of pupils and that a few of the teachers, including the head, did not seem to understand the principles of inclusivity. All smiles and right words on the surface at the school gate and during school performances, but apparently under the thumb of the wealthy village PTA. The school was by now notorious amongst those who had suffered under its snobbish, divisive attitudes and procedures. Children with extra needs were bluntly advised to go elsewhere, whilst others were branded naughty if they were kinesthetic learners who struggled to spend the required hours sitting quietly without fidgeting. Especially if they were children from the less well off households in the village as became evident when so much of this cohort found places in more welcoming nearby schools. Some villagers threw up their hands in horror at the Ofsted verdict, unable to deal with the shame of their child attending a school in special measures. Some even complained to Ofsted, such was their arrogance. So comfortable were they in their assumption they will always get their own way, they could not comprehend the possibility that they might not be able to hold sway with Ofsted, who, for all its faults, expects equality of treatment and equal opportunities for all children. As far as these villagers were concerned, their own child had thrived at the school and it couldn't and shouldn't be faulted. When she was feeling generous, Jenny could concede that maybe it wasn't that they didn't care about the children whose lives had been adversely affected by the school, it was simply that they couldn't comprehend life outside their own privileged existence and that other children had had their lives blighted by the school.

Incredibly to Jenny, the primary school operated after school clubs that had to be paid for. If parents couldn't pay, the child didn't get to do the club. There were no free clubs for children whose parents might not be able to afford to pay for them. It was as if the cost of living crisis hadn't reached the village's hallowed hedge boundaries, and if it had, and a child was from a less well off family, the teachers whispered about it confidentially as if the whole matter was somehow distasteful. Where were the free classes for pupils whose families lived on the breadline? Nowhere around here, that's for sure! 'Can't pay, can't attend' was the school's attitude. Yet this was a state school, not a private one, and state schools are surely supposed to open opportunities for children from all walks of life. Poorer children who might enjoy attending a club and who might discover new, life-changing talents were not given the opportunity. These after school clubs might well have been excellent, but they were not equitable and they were run for profit, often by well-off parents, not as a public service.

It was the pervasive attitude of 'us and them' that Ofsted condemned the school for. The common misconception that its 'rough' families who wreck lives and bully others was finally exposed in the village. While stereotypical bullies no doubt exist everywhere, many bullies masquerade as 'nice people' within a community. They are protected by wealth and privilege, and they are bullies because of it, having the power and the status to get what they want at the expense of others. It is this type of person that can go unchallenged in schools because of teachers' unconscious bias. Ofsted had exposed the inequalities and divisiveness that had been bound up with, if not directly linked to, the cause of Sam's unhappiness at school. But it was too late for Sam. Ofsted could not rescue him. The damage to him had been done and the course of his life was changed forever by it.

Because of the divisions at primary school, Jenny and Mike felt they had no choice but to send Sam to an out of catchment secondary school to give him a fresh start. It would have been far easier just to opt for the nearest comprehensive, and Sam himself wanted to go there initially, but it was in 'special measures' because of poor behaviour and the same kind of social divisiveness that had blighted the primary school, so to do so would likely have spelled disaster for Sam.

There had been two deaths by suicide of teenagers who had attended the school, and there were stories of similar teacher collusion with the glitterati as had happened at the village primary, so Jenny and Mike couldn't take the risk. Jenny and Sam took a look around the out of catchment comprehensive together, and, though they weren't massively keen, it seemed like a better bet for Sam. Two of his friends were going there so fingers crossed it would be okay, and there would be some familiar faces on the bus at least. Jenny and Mike felt hopeful for the future and prayed Sam might be able to start afresh in a place that might build his confidence rather than crush it. Secondary school started well for Sam. It's safe to say he had a lot of fun for the first few years. He did well at javelin too, and this gave him a bit of kudos. He made some new friends and led the life most young teens live, catching the bus into town, going to the cinema and generally hanging out. For a time, Jenny and Mike believed good times were here to stay. He'd got shot of the worst of the primary school crowd and appeared to be doing well. But sadly only for a time.

The thing with bullies is that they are relentless in their desire to make their victim's life a misery. Sam was in Year 9. It was a warm summer and the day of the village fair. Like with most villages, the community comes into the streets and the playing field, there are bands and stalls and a fun fair every year. Sam had always enjoyed it. He headed down to the fair with his friend happy and carefree, and it was only by chance that Jenny witnessed the incident that was to propel him into the worst years of his life, and condemn their family to years of misery.

She had been walking with Mike and Sam's little brother down Main Street to the village fair, when she saw the boy who had been Sam's sometime friend and often time tormentor at primary school jeering at him and goading him in front of a laughing crowd of others, mostly from his old primary school class. These were all kids who had transferred to the catchment school so Sam didn't come across them much any more. She could not hear what was being said, but the atmosphere of the scene wasn't nice.

The boy stood there looking cocky, a crowd of others behind him, while Sam looked pale and cowed.

Jenny's blood ran cold with fury.

The boy's eyes met hers and he smirked momentarily before turning to make off into the crowds, taking the others along with him.

Sam appeared shaken. Robbed of his dignity and self respect by whatever the taunts or threats had been, he took himself back home, thankfully with his friend who remained with him.

This event had a marked effect on Sam as it surely would on anybody, though he has never once spoken about it either then or many years later. If only, wished Jenny, Sam had felt able to ignore them and hold his head high. Not easy being one having to stand up to many, but if only he had told them to fuck off then proceed on his way to do exactly as he pleased. But he hadn't. He had, instead, absorbed the attack, just as he had absorbed the many confusing, unjust or cruel events that had littered his whole life. This boy had a long history of goading Sam, putting him down in front of others and having a laugh at his expense, so he'd obviously spotted an opportunity to do it again now, all these years later and out of nowhere. She wished Sam had it in him to not care and to fight back, but he seemed to be at the mercy of this idiot and his acolytes. No doubt the fact that this event had happened without warning or reason confused Sam and put him on the back foot. This pathetic little coward would probably have just said 'hi Sam' if they'd met alone, but he couldn't resist the urge to assert himself in front of a crowd. It made her blood boil. Always one to be proactive and deal with issues arising, she approached the boy's parents about what she had seen.

'But he likes Sam,' the mother had said, apparently genuinely bewildered. She was a nice woman who Jenny had always been on good terms with and she seemed to be genuinely concerned.

'That's not how it looked to me,' Jenny made clear. 'And while your son is out with his mates enjoying the fair, Sam has gone home.'

The mother said she would talk to her son but it amounted to nothing. The damage was done.

School continued until the end of year 9, but problems were starting to appear. Sam had lost trust in his friends. Some of them knew his old primary classmates who were now poisoning his social success at school. The kids who had been his friends through Years 7, 8 and most of 9 were starting to change. Social media has opened up the world for today's teenagers so that everyone knows everyone no matter what county secondary school they go to. There is no escape any more. Boys in his friendship group were going out at weekends and leaving him out, then coming to school on Monday mornings and talking about what a great time they'd had in front of him. Some of them played football with his old primary school classmates. They were meeting up at lunch breaks and excluding him from conversations. This kind of thing happens routinely in 'friendship groups' in schools across the country. Some members of each group wield power over others and there's always a victim. The 'popular' ones are the ones that call the shots because they, for one reason or another, have the power. But often, ironically, they are not really popular at all, they are feared and disliked.

Silly child's stuff, some teachers say, no doubt keen to get on with the job of teaching rather than having to sort out friendship group dynamics. Totally understandable, yet, Jenny wondered, how many of them would manage to go into work if they had to deal with deliberate social exclusion and routine humiliation? Would they cope with colleagues treating them as if they don't exist? No, of course not. Like any normal person, they would start to feel unsure of themselves and unhappy, and they would no longer want to go to work.

This kind of bullying is particularly confusing because oftentimes the perpetrators actually do nothing observable to an onlooker. There is nothing they can be blamed for or called out on because with a smile and a shrug they deny it and there's no residual evidence to suggest otherwise apart from an anxious victim with their nerves in tatters from the mind games being played. Very different to being beaten up, which of course is terrible, but you know what happened. With social exclusion, the victims are deliberately left confused, insecure and on the back foot, unable to explain what's going on and too embarrassed to show their face. It amazes Jenny that children are expected to tolerate situations no adult would be expected to put up with at work, and in a place from which there is no escape. From 8.30 am to 3.15 pm young people are trapped in school with hundreds and hundreds of others, some hostile, most indifferent and some, if you're lucky, friendly. They are expected to navigate often bewildering and exhausting dynamics that shift hourly, present themselves in a way that does not attract negative comments and, as if that isn't exhausting enough, learn in classes of 30 or more individuals each with their own attitude, learning ability and personality. At school, there is literally no escape once you're in and the gates slam shut. No wonder so many young people liken school to prison. In her day, Jenny could walk home for lunch. Not any more. Once in, that's it, and often you're not even allowed out if you feel ill in case you miss out on 'learning time.' Such restrictive, controlling circumstances must inevitably have a detrimental psychological effect.

Sam moved tutor groups at the end of Year 9, so Jenny and Mike hoped things would improve at the start of Year 10 and that recent issues had been nothing more than a glitch. School had been reluctant to allow this to happen in case it 'set a precedent', but if a pupil struggles to attend, school is required to make an effort to help them so Jenny persuaded them to swap Sam into his chosen group. Sam had a friend in the new tutor group so surely he'd be fine. Betty was still calling for him in the morning every day so things appeared to be back on an even keel. When the start of year 10 came things seemed to be okay for the first term. But soon Sam's friend, also a boy on the fringes of the friendship group, took to trying to keep in with the 'populars', and part of this necessitated sidelining Sam in favour of doing what was necessary to save himself. For all the issues Sam faced, he was not one to suck up, and could not fall in with behaviour he disliked. But now his friend was attempting to ingratiate himself with the populars. It's everyone for himself in the pack mentality, and if you don't fall in and comply you're on your own, especially in those crucial developmental years of Year 9, 10 and 11.

Jenny and Mike were worried about what was going on at school, which was supposed to be a place of 'in loco parentis' where young people are safeguarded but in reality seemed to enable a confusing, toxic underworld the teachers apparently had no idea about. Sam refused to participate in anything he felt uncomfortable with and this set him apart from others. He hated social media, liked his private life to be private, didn't enjoy getting laughs at other people's expense and felt uncomfortable with macho antics. At school nothing is private, everything is public business. Such an environment is not conducive to people who prefer their privacy. If someone is off for a day or two everyone wants an explanation for why. If an explanation is not forthcoming, rumours are circulated and you're accused of skiving. Social media accounts are stalked and commented on, WhatsApp groups routinely involve cruel bullying. Every teenager has been part of a group chat that turns nasty. The chat starts off fine, then group members start talking about someone present as if they are not there and vicious things are said. Jenny has heard of kids being told by multiple group members to kill themselves, for example. She couldn't imagine how it must feel to have to go into school the next day after such a thing had happened, having to sit next to the same kids in lessons and come across them in break times. But it happens day in, day out before the victim can't stand it any more and stops going to school. It's a commonplace occurrence, but they don't tell. Rule number one: never tell.

None of this was articulated by Sam, and none of this happened to him as far as she knew, but Jenny learnt from her younger son and his friends what went on at school and in social media and chat groups. Jenny was proud of Sam, who knew his own mind and had his own boundaries. It occurred to her years later that in bowing out of school he was in actual fact maintaining his own standards, and what seemed like a failure to school was actually a dignified defiance to be admired. But this realisation came much later, when the agonising years of school refusal and 'shut down' had long passed.

There was also talk of knives being taken into school. Jenny and Mike only got wind of this indirectly, because Sam would not tell them anything about what went on in school. He never named anyone or

spoke directly about issues facing him. Nothing would make him open up. Rule number one was never talk, especially to teachers or parents. If Sam ever let his worries slip it came in the form of vague questions.
'If someone came into school with a knife, would they be able to track me down?' He had once asked, the closest they had got to gaining an insight into his worries.
Jenny and Mike were horrified. What on earth had happened, or was happening, at that school? Why would he ask such a thing? Had he been threatened? Had he seen things on the news or on social media? Or was something actually afoot at his school? Possibly it was both, because social media crazes spread and become reality everywhere very quickly. It seemed to be worry about a potential knife attack that had the most profound effect on Sam, and this put paid to any return to school. But exacerbating this worry was his feeling of lack of autonomy and the pressure of being trapped at school. Sitting in the deputy head's office, he listened silently, eyes cast down to the floor, while she explained how he could protect himself against so called 'County Lines' by telling a teacher about anything suspicious, and how there had never been a knife attack at this school as yet. A poster on the wall confirmed a police visit to school to warn about such dangers in assembly.
Jenny had sat alongside Sam and listened to all of this. Even she could recognise the ridiculousness of

the deputy head's words. It was evident that Sam was too tense in the school environment to find comfort in what Mrs Jones had to say, and even Jenny knew that no self respecting teenager would dream of 'telling a teacher' about someone carrying a knife in school. To do so would be certain social death, and with it a probable serious beating or knifing. She was pretty sure he had no idea what 'County Lines' was either. Mrs Jones's advice was pointless though well meaning, only confirming her cluelessness about real life for teenagers, certainly for Sam, in her school and modern life for teenagers in general. Sam was frozen. Anxiety manifested itself in his face and posture. He was at the frontline and nothing Mrs Jones had said had helped; in fact, it had made things worse because she had inadvertently confirmed how out of touch she was. Jenny had wanted to weep with anguish seeing him like this, and she knew now there was no going back.

They'd sat in silence on the way home from this fateful meeting. Though presenting a pleasant face, the deputy had again hinted at fines for non attendance. She was also happy to suggest that they might like to change schools or take Sam off roll. Sam had tried a reduced timetable but this had not worked because he was too worried about being seen coming in late. He had been asked to try the school counsellor again but in order to get to her new room he had to walk past his old form room and risk being seen by his classmates, and therefore judged by them, which he couldn't do. Jenny knew they were running out of options.

School did not understand why the special measures they had put in place to help Sam had not worked. As far as they were concerned, they had tried to help but he hadn't been responsive, and that meant they viewed his inability to come to school as defiance, especially as he did not have a mental health diagnosis.

But Jenny could see as clear as day why the plans to get Sam back into school hadn't worked: they were school's plans, not Sam's. Well meaning but clueless teachers had come up with ideas to help Sam - but without checking with him how workable they were. Of course he couldn't walk past his form room full of peers on the way to the counsellor! He was terrified of being seen. For Sam, being seen was the worst thing imaginable. To walk past them all to see a counsellor would be like asking a self conscious introvert to walk down a catwalk. It would be an impossible task for him. But he couldn't explain any of this to the powers that be, he just remained silent. And even if he could have found the words to explain why their plans were impossible for him to follow, would they have listened? All his experience of school told him they operate to their own agenda even when they were trying to help him, and they would not understand him even if he did have the power of words to explain. So he remained silent, impotent and passively defiant.

Jenny was rapidly developing a strong understanding of the way schools work, for better or worse. She knew in her heart that fining the family of a child too anxious to attend school was inappropriate, as was any attempt to off roll and therefore wash their hands of their responsibility to help him. But she also knew such measures were inevitably going to come their way if Sam did not start attending because unfathomably, this is what schools do to force anxious children back into school.

So much easier to persecute the vulnerable and try to force them to conform rather than deal with the root of the problem, Jenny thought. Schools would then have to take on the 'popular kids' from families they'd rather keep on board. They'd also have to admit that the kinds of kids who relentlessly make others' lives miserable at school do so not because they are 'going through' something themselves, but because they get a kick out of it or for dares. They enjoy the status it brings. They want to stay on top. This is not what teachers want to believe or admit, because to do so would mean admitting that some kids enjoy doing unkind things just as some adults enjoy doing unkind things, and this would pour cold water over current 'restorative justice' practices. Schools would also be forced to reflect on their restrictive practices such as locking toilets during the school day and forcing young people to wear absurd, uncomfortable uniforms, and they aren't about to do this in a hurry. When she was summoned to a 'crux' meeting with the deputy head, Jenny steeled herself to tell Mrs Jones in no uncertain terms that she was not going to be threatened with fines. She also insisted more help be put in place for Sam.

'I'm not going to be beaten into submission by a school that doesn't understand, or want to understand, the nightmare that my son is living through,' she had said. It took all the courage she could muster but it had to be done. Too often in school meetings she had been outnumbered and talked down. Now, she was determined to stand her ground. She owed it to Sam.

Jenny's stand had surprised Mrs Jones. Schools up and down the country routinely issue fines for non attendance against anxious children for whom school is an unkind, unsafe place. These children are very often then off rolled because parents are tricked into thinking homeschooling is their only option in the face of fines, and their children are left without an education if their parents or carers then struggle to provide it for one reason or another. Such parents' lives are turned upside down when they find themselves criminalised. Many parents have to give up work, many have breakdowns, many divorce under the pressure of it all. Jenny hadn't known the extent of the school system's malfunction in the early days of Sam's breakdown, but a few months down the line, her understanding was building after undertaking research and finding out about other young people who were also refusing to attend school. At the time, somehow finding the strength to make a stand, Jenny was not going to let her own family be torn apart by this injustice. She was going to fight for Sam and win, no matter what dirty tricks were played on her. She had formulated an idea about the manipulations that go on behind the scenes in schools and councils to force children into school, and, driven by desperation, she had built the confidence to be able to face them head on.

'It is not Sam's fault that he cannot come into school, goodness knows he has tried hard enough and so have we. I will not be threatened by fines because I will not pay them. Furthermore, I will consult about where you have fallen down in your statutory duty to help my son. I insist you fulfil your obligations to him.' She'd announced something like that on her return to face Mrs Jones, and was quite taken aback at her own forcefulness.

'Well,' the deputy had replied, 'we can make a referral to CAMHS, but the waiting list is a mile long and it might be a year until he's seen.

'Yes please.' She had heard of CAMHS but knew very little about it. However, Jenny now knew that unless Sam secured an official diagnosis of school phobia, which Sam suffered from clear as day even to a lay person's eye, there would always be pressure exerted on him to attend school, and only CAMHS could provide such a diagnosis.

And what about his education?' Jenny pushed, keeping things business-like rather than emotional, even though she was shaking.

'He will have to keep trying to come into school, Mrs Blakes. For our part, we have tried a range of measures to help Sam, and I now feel it's time for Sam to push himself a little more. We can start off by arranging for him to come in for his favourite lesson,' she had replied.

'I think we both know that will be impossible for Sam,' Jenny had replied, firmly. 'He's been trying and failing to do exactly this for months, so pressuring him to try again is only going to reinforce his sense of failure every time he has to turn around and head for home, which is every time he tries to come into school..so what's the point? Surely it's time to come up with something better than that now.'

Mrs Jones had not offered an alternative to school but agreed to refer him to CAMHS. They arranged to meet the following week with the aim of sorting out Sam's schooling, but Jenny could tell Mrs Jones was still angling to get Sam back into mainstream classes despite the overwhelming amount of evidence to suggest the unsuitability of this.

Jenny felt emboldened because she had heard word of mouth about an establishment that might be able to offer help to Sam. Immediately, she contacted the small, local college aligned with CAMHS she'd been told existed locally but which wasn't widely known about because it was relatively new. She asked to speak to a CAMHS worker via the single point of access, a provision she had recently been told about. She got through easily and explained Sam's situation and the school's inadequate approach.

It was the best thing she could have done.

Not only did the CAMHS professional really listen to Jenny, but he also recognised the urgency of the situation. Within two days, the incredible mental health worker had contacted Mrs Jones to recommend she offer Sam an online teaching programme because he was not able to attend school and this was not likely to change. He reiterated to Mrs Jones that Sam was an extreme case and he would absolutely not recommend a push to attend school because to do so could lead to significant harm for him as he was clearly school phobic. He also offered Sam immediate drop in mental health support. Jenny was staggered at the rapidity of help now coming Sam's way and was obviously extremely grateful. They had struggled for so long she couldn't quite believe that Sam was now going to get the help he needed.

'He can try online schooling on the recommendation of CAMHS,' the deputy head conceded in the following meeting. It's expensive, but we should be able to fund the core subjects until the end of Year 11.'

Jenny accepted without hesitation and relayed the offer to Sam. He himself said nothing, or maybe he shrugged a consent, but within a week he was home learning online four days a week. School had also offered Sam a one day a week funded place at a local college on the recommendation of CAMHS, who believed it would be a low threat portal for Sam to access the outside world and build his confidence. CAMHS sessions started two weeks later.

Jenny was overwhelmed with gratitude for CAMHS for instigating swift action for Sam. Without them, school would still be pushing for Sam to go back to school. It all happened at once after what seemed like a stroke of luck in her decision to contact single point of access directly. Sam had been very, very lucky. But what would have happened if she'd never heard of the college and single point of access? Unfortunately, for many young people the waiting list for CAMHS is years, as Mrs Jones had pointed out. Even if they are suicidal or self-harming it can be a while until they are seen, depending on whereabouts in the country they live. Jenny and Mike were relieved that things were now moving quickly for Sam, though at this point they had no idea that he had been self-harming. Sam was probably as low as it is possible to be after spending months in bed locked into his own private torment. But now that the threat of fines and the pressure to go back to school were over, he could start on his road to recovery. Mrs Jones became more relaxed and friendly now that Sam's alternative schooling had been officially requested by CAMHS, so Sam and the whole family could relax into a new way of doing school.

The online education wasn't perfect, but at least he was tentatively doing it, relieved the threat of being forced into school was no longer hanging over him. Undoubtedly, the remaining GCSE year was a lonely one for Sam, but at least he was starting to recover. He also had a purpose to his days, something to get up for. It was obvious that Sam was barely engaging with his online lessons, but he was getting up and dutifully sitting at the computer every morning so he was at least learning something. Better than not getting any education at all, Jenny supposed. The college, however, was life-changing for Sam. It wasn't an easy start, by any means. It took all Jenny had to get him into the car to get him to the site, and when they drove through the college gates he hid in the back of the car and refused to get out like he always did when going to new or what he perceived to be 'risky' situations. Because this had been the pattern in the dying days of school, Jenny had anticipated it and asked a friend who was visiting the college that day to come to the car and coax him out. Myra had years of experience of working with recalcitrant teenagers, be they anxious, naughty or somewhere in between, so if anyone was going to get him out of the car it would be her. The plan had worked. Expertly and patiently she coaxed him out and Sam went with her to meet one of the teachers and look around. Watching him go, Jenny's eyes pricked with tears. Tears of pride that he had found the courage to leave the safety of his room to take this risk, and tears of relief that he was outside experiencing life rather than holed up in his room alone with his thoughts.

Myra had only needed to be at the college waiting for Sam that once. Subsequently, he was able to get out of the car and make his way in by himself. It seems he sensed he was safe, away from the crowds, noise and potential threat of school. He attended the college for the rest of the year then went on to complete a BTEC over the next few years, gaining a top grade. By design, Sam's BTEC did not involve written examinations, it was a modular course where his hands-on ability was assessed. Jenny knew Sam was too risk averse due to past experiences to be able to sit an exam just yet, so the continual assessment method was perfect for him, allowing him to access success in a genuine way. Sam made a couple of friends on his course and he liked the teachers who were kind to him and understood anxiety. Slowly but surely, Sam's mental health was recovering and his self-esteem was growing. This is what he needed: a quiet, calm learning environment where he could learn a range of valuable life skills alongside others who needed a similar approach. College was life-changing for Sam.

CAMHS had been instrumental in driving forward this new way of doing education for him, so as far as Jenny was concerned CAMHS involvement had been invaluable. Upon driving him to his first CAMHS session, however, Sam once again hid in the back of the car and wouldn't get out. But his CAMHS worker came out to the car and was eventually able to coax him in, just like Myra had been able to. It was as if he sensed the genuineness so allowed himself to be coaxed. Sam liked his CAMHS worker, and once the initial connection was made and the trust was there, Sam benefitted from his input.

But Sam wasn't entirely honest with CAMHS. Because the meetings were confidential, Jenny never knew exactly what they talked about, but she suspected and later found out that Sam didn't fully open up. He didn't admit many feelings and he didn't talk freely about school. Jenny wondered if maybe he was ashamed of having to leave school. Whatever the reason, he couldn't delve as deep as his counsellor wanted him to go. Jenny guessed Sam couldn't face up to everything that had happened to him because of the shame he carried deep down. He just wasn't ready to open up. But this is only a guess. Sam has never said.

Around this time, Jenny realised that it is likely shame that keeps struggling teenagers silent. Shame keeps them from admitting to parents, CAMHS, teachers and even to themselves that there is anything wrong. And fear of more shame keeps them from ever telling teachers about bad things that happen to them at school. The level of trust needed to lay themselves bare to a teacher is simply not achievable for most teenagers. 'Tell the teacher you are being bullied' is a pointless and laughable decree, as is 'tell the teacher if you don't understand.' What teenager trying to hold on to their last shreds of dignity would risk everything by telling a teacher they are being bullied? All young people know about schools' ways of attempting to solve relationship problems, and they understand it can never end well for them if they tell. The backlash online and repercussions in and out of school would be huge, and things would become immeasurably worse.

One day when Sam was out at college, Jenny ventured in to clean out his room. Fiercely private and covetous of his personal space, the job was long overdue. Picking her way through the sweet wrappers, drink cartons and screwed up bits of paper that were strewn under his bed, she came across an old school note book amongst the bits and pieces. Picking it up to move it rather than look inside, her attention was roused when the pages fell open to reveal what looked like sketches inside, so she took a closer look. What she saw made her blood run cold. Shaking, she turned the pages to reveal horror after horror.

Page after page of pen drawn images scratched into the paper with jagged black lines. Some of them hanging from a noose, others with slit wrists pouring blood. Each image seemingly an illustration of unspoken personal anguish spilling onto the page - an impotent call for help from a young man locked into a mental breakdown. All of the images in a cartoon style but with dark crosses in place of eyes. The shock of seeing these images had a profound effect of Jenny. Uncontrollable sobs convulsed through her she was so overcome by the mental anguish held within these pages. Such overwhelming loneliness. He must have been scratching these images in the days when he had shut himself in his room and not come out, in the days he could not bear to go to school, in the days he had been seeking to erase himself feeling others had erased him. Or maybe he had sketched them at school. Had he scratched these images in the hours he'd spent locked in a loo cubicle rather than going to science? Here before her was Sam's school memoir in place of the year book he never featured in. What a damning indictment of school.

At that time, shakily clutching Sam's memoir of horror, Jenny thought she would never recover from

the shock of her discovery. In his concluding report, issued once Sam's 12 weeks of therapy were up, Sam's CAMHS worker wrote there were no suicidal thoughts and there had been no self harm. But was this really true if these sketches were anything to go by? Jenny had just uncovered Sam's innermost turmoil from school days, unspoken but conveyed in images, and Jenny had seen his scratches.
Superficial cuts on his thighs and arms. Seen quite by accident, without Sam's intention.
'Hang on, what are those?' She had said, reaching out to stop him pulling down his sleeve.
'The dog scratched me,' he said, quick as a flash, shrugging. A good liar? Jenny looked hard at him but had to let it go. For now it was enough that he knew she had seen his scratches. She wouldn't push but would keep an eye on things. But surely CAMHS should have known if Sam was self-harming. Didn't they have ways of knowing or finding out without having to rely on being told? They must know young people don't always tell the truth or aren't able to tell. It appeared not so, like with so many things in Sam's mental health history, he only admitted to self-harm much later, and only very briefly. And when Jenny told Sam she had come across his notebook whilst cleaning his room he'd said 'oh, that old thing. Leave it mum, it's nothing. Just Manga type stuff. I liked the style.'

Maybe he was right. Jenny had leafed through plenty of Manga comics and books and knew the genre, though Sam did not open up about his private worries at all and wouldn't have admitted to the drawings being a release of personal pain. It was the same with the knives at school riddle, denied by Mrs Jones who, in the same breath, warned of the dangers of County Lines.

'Oh yeah, everyone had knives at school,' someone's son had announced so casually Jenny could barely remember when. It was as if this was common knowledge.'No one says anything because you don't. Who is gonna tell teachers shit like that?'

'Did they, Sam?' Jenny asked when it seemed like a good moment.

Sam shrugged. 'Can't remember.'

Golden rule number one: tell nothing.

Months later, Sam had some outdoor work experience. It was going well for the first few days and Sam was getting good feedback from his mentor. But then Jenny received a call. One of those calls where her blood ran cold because she instantly knew that something was wrong. Her heart sank.

'Mum, I can't do it, I have to come home. Come and get me.' Sam's voice was scared and urgent.

'What's happened, Sam? What's going on?' Quizzed Jenny, scared to hear the answer but ready to act.

'Mum, they want me to use a big knife to cut open sacks. I'm freaked out and I don't want to.'

Jenny could hear the panic in his voice and she thought he was likely having a panic attack, possibly brought on by a flashback to schooldays. Instantly, she headed for the car.

'Don't worry, you don't have to do anything you don't feel comfortable doing, so just walk away, tell them you have a migraine then stand outside the gate and wait for me. I'll come now.'

She'd left work and driven at speed to collect him. There he was, looking ashen faced and stiff like he had when she'd seen him walking down the school corridor. She hugged him and brushed the floppy hair from his eyes. 'You're alright now, Sam. You did the right thing to call me. Don't worry, let's just get you home. We can sort things out later.'

After a few minutes silence on the drive home, she decided it might be a good moment to ask him about the scratches she'd seen on his arm. 'Those weren't dog scratches on your arm were they, Sam?'

His eyes darted to hers uncertainly, but he knew there was no escape.

He said nothing but he shook his head and she'd driven on in tears with silence between them.

Later, when he'd had time to think about it and prepare to have a chat, Jenny pressed Sam on the matter of scratching and found, unsurprisingly, that he had started doing it when he was in school.

'It was only light scratching and made me feel better at the time, mum. It was like physical pain was easier to deal with and I could have some kind of control. I don't do it any more. It passed when I no longer had to go in. It was only a phase, almost like it was compulsory at the time.

'Why didn't you tell CAHMS, Sam?' She had pleaded. 'Mum, not being funny but they weren't going to be able to help me with that. I didn't tell him about a lot of things. I knew that none of the strategies he'd give me would help, and that if I told him everything it would only make things worse. I just had to wait until school was over, then I could start again. CAMHS can't change school.'

Jenny had stared at him in stunned silence. He had been so Impressively self-aware even in the midst of his mental breakdown. She also knew he was right. For Sam, when a situation was over that was it, he didn't want to have to think about it again. The last thing he would want to do is dredge up stuff about school to tell CAMHS because as far as he was concerned it was over and he therefore didnt have to think about it again.

Jenny had had to explain to the work experience placement that Sam would be fine as long as he was not required to work with knives or other sharp instruments at this particular stage in his life. Understandably, they didn't see it that way and he was instructed not to return. They did say he would be welcome to reapply in the future because he was great, but ultimately, Jenny sensed they saw him as a liability and Sam would have to accept he wasn't going back. Sam's mentor did not want to have to think about anything other than getting on with the job, which was fair enough. Sam had enjoyed the work and he was good at it. And she was certain he would have been fine, too, if they'd allowed him to stay the course. Jenny trusted Sam's judgement. He had never suffered with an impulse to self-harm since he had left school and she knew he was fine in himself bar the occasional intrusive thought or flashback such as this one. She knew he was dealing with the aftermath of school and she had absolute faith that he would get better once the trauma of school had properly passed. All that was needed was more time and distance.

If only..if only. Jenny and Mike were now living with too many if onlys. If only Sam had had a nice primary teacher when it mattered and a decent primary school, if only Sam had not 'failed' in school football and cycling so publicly, if only Sam's interests had been valued as much as anyone else's, if only his identity hadn't been negated, if only Sam had found space to feel comfortable and be himself at secondary school. If only school and the people within it had been calmer and less unpredictable. If only.

Jenny and Mike sometimes felt that when anxiety affects a family, others, especially school professionals and some 'friends', whisper behind the scenes that the child is too sensitive, the mother is too protective or the family itself must somehow be dysfunctional. Jenny would never forget the time when Sam, then in Year 8, had returned home from school enraged, slamming the door behind him and gulping down heavy sobs of fury.

'What on earth has happened?' She quizzed, concern coursing through her veins.

'That twat stole my fucking bag and chucked it around the bus,' he shouted. 'Fucking arsehole, fucking dick.'

'Which twat, Sam?'

Armed with the knowledge of which boy had done this to Sam, she drove to his house and confronted the mother. They had maintained a friendly relationship over the years despite her son's behaviour. This was one of the boys who'd goaded Sam at primary school periodically. Unfortunately, he had transferred to the same school as Sam so Sam had to deal with him on the school bus.

'I want to speak with your son myself,' she'd thundered to the mother.

The boy appeared at the door behind his mother, a smirk smeared across his face.

'If you EVER do that again,' she said forcefully, pointing a finger with intent, 'I will see to it that you are banned from the school bus. They make it quite clear they will not tolerate that kind of behaviour, and I will make sure of it. Do I make myself crystal clear?' The smirk vanished and the mum did not look happy, but Jenny was past caring. This little bully had got away with his nasty antics in the past and she was going to make sure it didn't happen again.

The mother had had to concede her son had been in the wrong.

'It was only a joke,' she'd complained to begin with, as if her boy was the one who was being wronged. 'Sam's not laughing,' Jenny had retorted, and the mother was forced to shrug a grudging consent.

The boy's father had called her later that evening. 'A bit of an over reaction,' he'd reasoned, voice patronising with the soft veil of indifference. 'Boys will be boys, he was just having a laugh. No need to come screaming round my house.'

'With all due respect, it's not funny when the other person is not laughing,' she'd retorted. 'It's bullying. And I wasn't screaming. If you don't teach children their actions are wrong, they won't become nicer people. They won't learn that they don't own the world, they share it with others. They won't learn empathy.'

Such is the prevailing attitude of school professionals too. Bullied kids are expected to suck up endless humiliations and bounce back as if to say: 'I don't mind how much you kick me, I'll just put up with the nasty things you find funny'. Schools ask the impossible with the fashionable restorative justice approaches they use. There's only so much a self-respecting teenager can take before rejecting a bully-enabling school for good. Imagine being forced to sit in the same room alongside someone who has stolen your bag and thrown it around the bus thinking it's funny, and listening to them lie about being sorry because they are playing the restorative justice game required by teachers. Imagine being forced to accept the apology of a bully you know isn't sorry, and you know comments are being posted about you in WhatsApp chats and your peers are laughing about you behind the scenes. This is why Jenny went to speak to the boy and his mum directly. Because consequences for bad actions are increasingly few and far between in schools and victims' situations are so often made worse in and after restorative justice meetings.

Once Sam was up and running with online learning and his day at the college, things seemed to settle down for a bit. At least he was getting out and interacting with other young people his age. But there remained an air of sadness about him. There was a distance in his eyes that told you he was still lost. Sam got through college, achieved the highest possible grade for his BTEC, and made some new friends. Past experience had taught him to be guarded, probably even if he didn't need to be. That said, he encountered no problems with anyone and he got on with everyone, so he was learning to how to navigate social situations successfully in college, which was a safer and less frantic environment than school. Three years had passed since the start of college, so there were always going to be ups and downs over time, but Sam's sense of purpose and worry about having to do a final year presentation built in his mind.

Though he was undoubtedly getting better because he was participating in life and had a steady social life, Sam also found himself staying up all night and sleeping all day. Jenny wondered if this was his way of avoiding having to cope with too much social time or college. Or maybe it was fairly typical teenage behaviour which is these days seen as a problem and medicalised. Some of her school friends had been nocturnal. Isn't it a way of life that suits the teenage body clock? At least Sam had the excuse of being tired when he wanted to withdraw for a while if he had been awake all night. Sam had lost interest in the final year of his course so this probably didn't help. Jenny and Mike advised him to stay at it because college had been so good for him, but towards the end of college Sam felt he needed the help of anti depressants to get through life. The doctor prescribed Sertraline with the aim of helping him sleep and settling his growing depression. Sam took it but it didn't seem to help much. The dosage was upped further and Sam's depression finally seemed to ease as he became more 'blank.'

For a year, Jenny, Mike and Sam's little brother lived under the weight of Sam's depression and apparent flatness. Though he still maintained the bare minimum of college work so as not to completely crash as he had done previously, the whole family became a family in mourning again. Sam's brother, from whom he'd once, all those years ago, been inseparable, now found himself living almost as a single child again, eating with his parents whilst Sam ate upstairs, going out for haircuts on his own when he'd always used to go with Sam. Unlike Sam, he still went to school and, unlike Sam, was apparently doing OK. There were the same issues with toilets, friendship groups and detentions, but because his early school experience had been better, and his cohort of peers was more balanced and mixed, he had an easier time of it. For Sam, college had begun to tail off and increasingly his days would be spent in bed, just as they had been in the first weeks and months of school refusal. After all, he'd lost all his school friends and was still adrift, despite accessing so much success at college. Also, the damaging experiences he'd suffered throughout school were not going to simply evaporate. He was certainly on the road to recovery, but he still had a way to go. There were times when Jenny feared it was never going to end and Sam would never fully recover. 'Life seems to stand still', she thought. It was a particularly bleak day and she was out for a walk in the woods with her dog. Sam hadn't gone in for his class and was still in bed at home. She had allowed her mood to sink into despair and was feeling self-pitying. 'We are held hostage by all that has happened to Sam and all the damage done. We can't move on, all we do is exist.' She spoke the words out loud to no one in particular, but her beloved dog was by her side and she always seemed to understand. Many of her friends had gone by the wayside and the ones who were left were not people she wanted to open up and admit things to. The one friend who did know all about Sam's school trauma and the struggles he'd faced had turned her back on Jenny as if she might be contaminated by her. Never checked in with her to see if she was ok, stopped sending Christmas cards and suggesting meeting up for coffee. Erasure. This is what happens when life falls apart: people don't want to know. They don't want the hassle in their busy lives. Having said that, Jenny admitted to herself, she too had stopped wanting people around, and she couldn't open up to talk to anyone about Sam if she wanted to. The words wouldn't come. What would she say? But she had called The Samaritans on that particular day. Sitting in her car in a lane out in the fields, loyal dog in the passenger seat by her side, she sobbed her heart out to a Samaritans volunteer, a complete stranger. .

'I have no reserves left,' she sobbed. 'I work, earn money, pay bills, and worry about my son who is taking antidepressants. I live in a constant state of terror that something awful will happen. I don't sleep and I'm exhausted. That's all I do, day in day out. I am existing in a state of high alert. I'm just so tired. I just don't think I can keep on going.' Jenny could feel the despair pouring out of her and it was a relief to let it flow.

'I can't say anything that will make you change your mind,' the Samaritan had told her when her hour was up. 'But I hope our conversation has been of use to you.'

Though the Samaritan had sounded kind at times, Jenny was painfully aware that the woman didn't actually care what became of her. Despite her evident anguish, Jenny gained the impression she was speaking to a woman who had volunteered to work for the charity because she was a nice person who wanted to do good, but neither heart nor soul was there, and that's what Jenny needed on that day.

'Thank you for your time,' she said blankly but managing to be polite, knowing she would never again reach out to this well meaning vacuum. The phone call had reinforced her feeling of aloneness and lack of support even when she had reached out for it. But at least now she felt irritation rather than despair, so in its way the conversation had given her a jolt in the right direction.

Jenny didn't take her own life that day. The Samaritan had in one way cemented her aloneness but in another way galvanized her resolve. She summoned her life's purpose from the despair that had engulfed it: to live on and care for her beloved children. She had to pick herself up and dust herself down because she had to support Sam until he was better, and until he and her youngest had found their paths in life. Of course she wanted to see them both into adulthood because she loved them so very, very much. There were going to be times when she felt she was running on empty and wished someone could be there to help her, but she could do it, she resolved. At least her beloved dog would be there by her side. Her faithful friend who listened patiently with undivided attention and non judgemental love, and got her out of the house for therapeutic walks in nature in the darkest of times, regardless.

Throughout Sam's struggle to make sense of the world of school that is one minute friendly then at a whim hostile, numerous 'experts' warned him, and Jenny and Mike as his parents, about the dangers of spending too much time online. They told Jenny and Mike that too much online time alters the brain and slows development. Limit him, they had instructed. Sam got his first X Box in Year 6, relatively late by today's standards. Like with most boys, gaming rapidly became a way of life, though he also went out and about and participated in family life. Jenny and Mike did not struggle to limit his time online, though as time progressed he played for longer and later into the evening. This, probably, was simply a part of growing up and becoming more independent.

Online, Sam tended to meet friends he knew in real life rather than reach out to new people elsewhere in the world. Jenny and Mike kept an eye on how Sam's online life was developing and there seemed to be few issues with it, though like most parents they did worry because it's a realm neither of them had any understanding of. The X Box had provided Sam with a safe new world in which he could experiment and play, and he seemed to have it under control.

However, it was when school had got really bad for Sam and his outer world had felt too unsafe for him to participate in that the X Box became his saviour. He couldn't cope with the pressure of having to attend the alienating school environment and all school forced him to deal with, but he was happy spending time online, building characters, exploring new worlds and pursuing other imaginative activities.

School, CAMHS and psychologists continued to warn of the dangers of spending too much time online, but Jenny and Mike could see this brave new world, largely unexplored and certainly misunderstood by older adults professing to be experts, was going to be the saving of Sam. In the dark, cruel years ahead, Sam, at odds with confusing behaviours in the 'real world', could access and control another world where he could flourish and feel safe. Jenny was in no doubt that the X Box saved Sam. Even more than the antidepressants and CAMHS, the X Box had helped him withdraw but remain in the loop in a way that he could control. Jenny dreaded to think what might have happened to Sam if he wasn't able to access a social and creative online world. Would he have made it?

Jenny and Mike were issued with advice from professionals to turn the wifi off at night when 'Sam should be sleeping, not playing games'. They seemed to think that if the X Box was turned off he would magically fall asleep, as if it was the technology that was the problem. Jenny and Mike were made to feel like failures for refusing to limit Sam's online activity.

'Control your child's online behaviour,' the professionals had said, 'he has come to rely on it and this will damage him in the long run.' The Mental health experts and school professionals considered it to be a matter of safeguarding. Too many potential dangers online that cannot be monitored, they warned. And too much disruption to day to day life. But Jenny was a parent who had a strong bond with her son and would never issue life-changing instructions without consulting him first. Sam had been overruled and undermined by professionals with no lived experience in the 'real world' for most of his life, so she was damned if she was going to do the same thing to him at home. She also knew Sam to be a person of strong morals and a good judge of character. He had, and still has, a well developed sense of right and wrong.

Perched on the rim of his bed, she had explained the professional advice to Sam and awaited his response.

'Mum,' he said, 'there is no 'real world'. My X Box life is just as real as school is. It helps me process stuff that otherwise would go round and round in my brain all night. It's just as real as anything else; it's just adults don't understand it because they don't do it.'

'They say it changes the way your brain works forever. It makes you less likely to be able to deal with people and outside life in general if you play too much.'

Sam rolled away and faced the wall.

'Mum, I'll be fine, just leave me be. What has outside life ever done for me?'

During his seven years of gaming, sometimes staying up most of the night to finish a game, Sam completed online learning and gained the qualifications he needed, attended college getting a distinction in his chosen field so becoming the college's highest achieving pupil on the course that year, completed work and got himself a public facing job. Slowly though haphazardly, Sam had proved that he could achieve when he was allowed to work in a way that

he could make sense of and gain autonomy. Jenny and Mike were under no illusions that life was hard for Sam because his trust in the outside world was in ribbons, but it was clear that Sam's gaming had had no detrimental effect on his ability to function. Rather, it allowed him to pace himself in a way that felt safe for him:
Complete an online lesson
Subsume myself in a game
Attend a day at college
Play a game all night when I can't sleep
Work a 6 hour day
Go to sleep for a few hours then play a game at night
Sam was building his confidence in a way that worked for him. He knew to trust himself and his family because trusting others had not served him well. Jenny and Mike could see that he was beginning to relax now that he knew they were completely on his side and would not be swayed by ill- informed professionals.
What impressed Jenny and Mike was that Sam was quite able to put his own boundaries around his online activity. They learned to relax, trust him to make his own decisions and leave him to enjoy his online life.
'I'm not stupid,' he had said from early on. 'I'm not an idiot. I know it all.'
By 'it all' he meant online safety.

They had been doubtful at first, listening at the bedroom door when they heard him talking to someone and doing what they could to keep an eye on what he was up to.

But ultimately Jenny was glad she had followed her gut instinct to listen to Sam and trust him. She learnt to endure the comments made by parents of mostly primary school children around the 'tight control' they had of their child's online activity.

'It's irresponsible to let them have more than two hours a day,' she had heard on plenty of occasions. 'If he hasn't turned his X Box off to join us for family dinner when he's told, he's banned the next day', one mum said.

Such statements made Jenny flinch. Such sure foottedness - good luck to them! She wondered if they would hold to such resolute standards if the online world was the only world their son or daughter felt safe from harm in, then quickly realised that they well might. Her heart sank for teenagers who were trapped, controlled and condemned to loneliness if their parents listened to the professionals and enforced the two hour rule. The truth is, there's a whole world of online gaming out there. It's a lifestyle. Young people connect, bond, share creativity and experiences online together in ways that most non-gaming adults don't understand.

For Jenny, this merciless imposition of an uncomprehending professional perspective onto teenagers they don't really understand, despite all their qualifications and status - maybe even because of them, can be harmful. The online world is a relatively new and rapidly growing one. For middle aged professionals who grew up with books and outside play time, the realm of online is often viewed with suspicion. Too passive, too violent, too easy, they think. Jenny and Mike themselves had once erred on the side of caution but they had re-educated themselves through Sam.

There was no doubt in Jenny's mind that Sam would have suffered more loneliness, boredom and despair if he had not had the creative outlet of his X Box and the freedom to use it at night when otherwise destructive thoughts swirled round in his brain. And, after years of playing a range of games, mostly world-creating fantasy realm epics, Sam remained a peaceful soul who loves animals and who can't stand violence.

Jenny and Mike had worried about Jake's online activity when he was a younger teenager just getting into it. They'd heard games involving misogyny and violence were popular with young men and were concerned that Sam might get into playing them. However, they needn't have worried because Sam was not interested in such games. The fullness of time, low-key monitoring and trust revealed he liked fantasy and creation games with mind-blowing graphics and mind opening opportunities to learn about different cultures, space and history.

For Sam, expressing his creative self online was more fun than games like football because he wasn't required to be competitive and he could be imaginative on his own terms. Many of his game as far as Jenny could tell involved strong, female protagonists, and the violence in the games, if there was any, was 'fantastical', nothing like the horrors that can be watched in 18 certificated movies - not his thing. And how much more fun it is to adopt personas and live out a fantasy game without the threat of failure. To Jenny's mind, such games are an extension of the role play games kids play when they're little when they dress up as Marvel heroes or their favourite book characters.

Sam also kept up with the news. He knew about the epidemic of fatal teen stabbings around the country. He knew that unsuspecting victims, the 'weak ones' in friendship groups are lured to lonely spots then stabbed to death for fun by people they thought were their friends. He knew that teachers in schools were clueless about the knives kids had hidden in their pockets and backpacks. This was his 'reality' and no amount of school sanctioned cajoling, fining or reassuring could persuade him to put himself at risk. It was fight or flight, and he had to fly because he disliked pack mentality, wasn't violent, and didn't particularly like much of the reality he saw around him at school where the dynamics between and within friendship groups was universally toxic. 'Online, Sam can simply leave or block if he comes across anything threatening,' Jenny said to Mike one day when she was having one of the many realisations she had had since Sam's crash out of school. 'He's in complete control, not at the mercy of people who want to do him harm or get him to do things he doesn't want to do' It was one of a succession of realisations that taught Jenny and Mike to trust Sam - trust in his ability to make his own decisions and therefore adjust to a different way of living. Now that Sam wasn't ever going back to school, Jenny had space to collect her thoughts and relax a little, and as she relaxed she began to piece together the jigsaw puzzle that formed a picture of how Sam's school refusal came to happen. Things that had not previously occurred to her began to come into view, and flashbacks illuminated the path to Sam's destination. It was a relief not to have to battle against what school felt Sam ought to do every day, although with that relief came the grief of losing their old way of life.

Jenny is sad at the tendency to medicalise anxiety and loneliness of the kind suffered by Sam and all the other young people for whom school is unfit for purpose. Instead of recognising harms done by, and within some school practices and approaches, and dealing with bullying that goes on within so called friendship groups in today's schools, the victims are medicalised: given diagnoses of anxiety and offered, if they are lucky, mental health support. The message they are therefore given is they are the faulty ones, when in reality they are simply removing themselves from humiliating or dangerous situations- surely a normal way to deal with threat. It is, in effect, fight or flight. After months of feeling alone with what happened to Sam, Jenny had started to come across more stories of school refusal, more tragic stories of previously happy children being crushed under the weight of judgment, bullying and not living up to expectations either in friendship groups or in the classroom. Jenny and Mike began to realise that far from being alone, Sam was part of an epidemic of teenagers whose only way of coping with a situation within which they were otherwise powerless, was to reject the outside world altogether. Harrowing stories of bewildered families struggling to make sense of what was happening to their once functioning, happy existence came her way. And for each one of these stories, the young person at the centre of it felt completely alone. None of these young people had any idea they were part of an epidemic, and none of the parents had a clue that their child was in fact part of an exodus marching away from mainstream schooling. Every one of those families likely felt as isolated as Jenny's family had become.

After Sam's involvement with CAMHS, it dawned on Jenny that he wasn't ill at all, he was simply doing what he had to do to deal with everything that had happened to him at school. CAMHS got his diagnosis of 'school phobia' absolutely right and for that she will be forever grateful. If it wasn't for the serendipitous meeting at single point of access, Sam's school would have made their lives a misery. But really, Sam wasn't what you would call ill. Once he had left school he started to get better. He was harmed by school, not ill. Jenny has heard of many instances where the school system actively validates and supports the bullies whilst medicalising the bullied by labeling them 'anxious'. When they start to feel better schools then try to force them back into school in order to 'fit in' and 'achieve'. The worst insult and misunderstanding levelled at Sam was that he had to 'be resilient.' By this, they meant he needed to 'push himself' and 'challenge himself' to 'get out of his comfort zone' and return to school. In other words, they expected him to buy into the school system and therefore uphold it, even though it was wrong. How convenient for them to turn the situation round on him, in effect making him feel more powerless and more of a failure than ever. The language developed by professionals rode roughshod over his decision to withdraw and his attempts to regain personal power. They tried to shame him into rejoining a failing system. 'If you don't find the resilience to come back to school now, you'll never learn and you'll always be the same,' the mantra went. Now that Sam, who never returned to school and whose parents did not buy into the professional language of shame, is a young man who functions well in society, he has well and truly proved them wrong.

'He is on the CAMHS waiting list,' they'd said at school. One box ticked. So much easier passing these kids on to CAMHS than getting to the root of the issue and actually changing the system to hold the bullies and dysfunctional structures to account. The toxicity of so called friendship groups constrains teenagers in the most incomprehensible ways.

'Just hang out with someone else,' Mike had said in the early days, and Sam would gape at him with incredulity.

'That's not how it works, dad.'

As the years had progressed, Jenny and Mike began to understand just how constrained teenagers are once they become part of a friendship group at school. It's the way schools work these days. Furthermore, you don't have to actually like everyone within your friendship group, a baffling fact that Jenny and Mike could not make sense of.

'But it's in the name - friendship group. Surely that means you are in a group because you like those people and have things in common to do with them!' Any parent might proclaim.

'Nope,' says any teenager you care to ask. 'It starts like that but once you're in it there's no moving, and most people end up bitching about each other or falling out.'

For some, this is all part of the game and to be expected. However, for those who value true friendship and loyalty, it's dispiriting and hard to deal with. Never knowing where you stand makes it difficult to go into school because you never know what awaits you. It's the luck of the draw. Will your friends be nice to you today or will they turn on you? Will they speak to you and include you or will you be left on the sidelines? Who knew? And the unpredictability of relationships and social dynamics plays havoc with your nerves.

The more time Jenny spent alone or with her family, the less Jenny wanted to go out. In the early days, she spent her time making sure Sam was OK and having his needs met as much as she was able to help him. She wanted to be at home with him because she knew if she went out she'd spend her time worrying about him and wanting to come home. Also, she liked and still likes being with her son more than she liked her friends and associates, and if he did ever come downstairs to chat or sit for a bit it made her heart soar higher than a night at the pub would have done.

Jenny found herself turning down party invitations and avoiding social situations.

'Oh, we'd love to come but we have something on that night.' The response to invitations began to come effortlessly.

The thought of attending a dinner party, once a monthly occurrence, became horrifying to her. It made her feel angry if Mike even suggested it.

'How can I go out and 'enjoy myself' knowing Sam is lying in bed at home on his own?' She'd retort angrily. 'YOU go if you care that much about seeing people who haven't even asked how he is.' Why would she want to spend time with anyone else over Sam, who she loved and cared about? Why would she choose to spend time with people who didn't care?

Apart from she wasn't often spending time with Sam. In reality she was running around after Sam, ensuring he had good meals delivered to his room, that he was safe from harm and that she was available should he ever need her. Her whole world had shrunk in order to protect him and take care of his needs. She didn't know it until Sam was obviously so much better years later, but she was lonely. Jenny felt Sam's brother was lonely too, though he never admitted it. She could tell he was lost and confused by his big brother's withdrawal and that he missed Sam, but he did get on with his life and was able to flourish and do his own thing. It is taking a long time to recover from the self-protective shell she built up around herself and turn the hatred she had felt for her friends into understanding and forgiveness. Jenny is only able to begin her road to recovery now she has seen Sam on the path to his.

During the years when Sam's life was in slow motion implosion and they had felt like they were the only ones to be going through the nightmare of school refusal, all around them life went on. Sam's friends progressed through school and continued on their expected trajectory through the world albeit disturbed for a while by lockdown.

Jenny had cried herself to sleep on a nightly basis when she wasn't listening in fear at Sam's door in case he cut his wrists or overdosed on antidepressants. How could their happy, normal family have come to this? What had they done wrong? What had they done to deserve any of this? She knows now that Sam would never have done either of these things because he had more control over his well being and actions than she had realised, but it was terrifying for her then. Operating in the unknown, Jenny's fears played on her mind and she lived in terror of the worst happening day in day out for years. She spent so long living in a state of hyper vigilance that was only now beginning to ease.

As the years passed and Jenny began coming across more and more stories of young people like Sam, it was as if Sam had gone from being the only boy in the world to have experienced the personal anguish of acute anxiety caused by school and societal restrictions to being a part of a modern epidemic. But the years of torment were over for him just as they were beginning for increasing numbers of others. Stories about teenagers like Sam began appearing in newspapers and items ran on the TV and radio with alarming frequency. And they mostly followed the same pattern. Lives apparently 'normal' in the early primary school years turned upside down and shredded by Year 9 or 10. Girls, boys and teens who identify differently in their hundreds of thousands now made ill, crushed under the weight of pressure to attend a school they couldn't cope with, forced to sit alongside those who ridicule, hate or bully them and be expected to function well within an increasingly straight jacketed system.

The more Jenny researched the issue of school avoidance, the more she came to realise that the families trying to cope with the pressures hers had navigated after Sam's mental collapse face an impossible uphill struggle to be heard, understood and respected. Head teachers are under pressure to maintain high attendance because their school is judged on attendance figures when Ofsted comes to call. Head teachers also believe that high attendance equates to high GCSE results, the higher the better, because top results show the school in a good light, at least in the headlines, which is what seems to matter most. Headteachers, along with other safeguarders working within the system, believe that school attendance protects children from the potential harms posed by county lines gangs and neglectful or abusive parents and carers. What they don't understand is the glaring reality that school causes more harm than good for an increasing number of children.

Jenny's lived experience was almost universally completely at odds with the mainstream mantra. Jenny and Mike read news article after news article about teenagers refusing to return to school after the Covid 19 pandemic and the various methods politicians devise to deal with the issue. There are, it is estimated, nearly a million children daily who are missing school. Behind the headlines, this mass rejection of mainstream schooling is made up of individual teenagers with their own tragic tale to tell, and they all feel alone. Mums, dads and carers who think they are the only ones; up to a million individuals who, unable to cope with the system, each feel the weight of failure crushing them as they struggle to find air. Unless parents choose to home school from the get go, of course, which is a separate demographic, and one similarly misunderstood and treated with suspicion by those bound up in a mainstream way of life and a mainstream way of thinking.

The more stories Jenny reads, the more she understands that each one started with rejection of the mainstream and all the ensuing chaos that involves. Uncomprehending teachers who turn up to work each day convinced their approach is right, Head teachers who can find no better answer than to threaten parents with fines if their child continues to refuse school, and an education minister who, driven by panic at the worsening national picture, issues the most ridiculous decree of all: head teachers should get in their cars and personally drive round to young people's houses, prise errant teenagers from their beds and drag them into school.

A motion picture of this very scene at her own front door played through Jenny's mind.

Knock knock

Jen: Hello

Head: Good morning Mrs Blakes, Why isn't Sam in school today?

Jen: He has been threatened with a knife by one of the many in his peer group who carry knives in your school. He has not got out of bed for two days and won't talk, only covers his head with his duvet and turns to face the wall. He rarely comes out of his room. When we have tried to drag him into school he is sick. We live in fear that he will harm himself.

Head: That simply isn't good enough, Mrs Blakes. I'm here to take him into school or you will face the full force of the law and face the appropriate fines. Let me in and show me to his room. I will then drive him to school myself and ensure he attends lessons,

especially maths and English, which are fundamental to students' life chances.
Jen: Well, Mr Head teacher, how about no? I'm afraid you will be driving back to school empty handed. Good bye and I sincerely hope you have a good day. Slam!
This scene and others like it often played through Jenny's mind. Scenes where she gave herself the opportunity to stand up to unfairness and call out the lies about schools that nobody speaks about - scenes of triumph against injustice! But when the curtains close on the scene and in her mind comes the fearful darkness again, she knows that the opportunity will never arise. She was one in a million parents and Sam was one in a million teenagers who were, and always would be, divided by the rule of laws made by those whom the system had served well. The trouble is, teenagers, even those who think they are a cut above or those who seek to set themselves apart in some way, want to fit in and be accepted by their group. And yet in today's schools it has become harder and harder to be a face that fits unless you are one of the 'populars'. Jenny has read account after account of teenagers whose stories are more or less identical to Sam's. They start off happy kids with parents who read them stories, take them to parties and provide a loving, stable home for them. There are almost imperceptible glitches, as yet unrecognised clues as to what is to come in the later

years of primary school, a couple of apparently settled years at secondary school and then.. wham! Life changes forever and the walls come tumbling down.

'This just cannot go on,' Jenny routinely complained to Mike. 'This epidemic of school refusal is a symptom of a social malaise of restriction, conformity and fear that British teenagers can't deal with, and shouldn't have to deal with. Since when did it all become so complicated?'

Jenny wonders if some issues around school refusal come down to restorative justice, the approach schools take to bullying. If a young person is caught bullying and told they have behaved badly and they will be punished one way or another, surely they themselves are given the opportunity to learn to be better and understand the harm they caused another. There is no equivocation. Verbal bullying, name calling and beating people up are nasty and harmful. Anyone caught doing such things should surely be told so, educated and punished. It's how children learn right from wrong. With RJ, however, it appears there's no such thing as right or wrong, only a different point of view. If a young person is caught beating the living daylights out of another young person in the school playground, teachers will be expected to find out why they did it; to understand and explain the bully's motivation as if they too are somehow a victim. This done, the perpetrator's motivation will be explained to the victim, who will then be expected to sit in a room with the person who beat, humiliated, taunted or terrorised them and accept their reason for doing so. Behind the forced apology from the bully will often be smirks and continued online abuse, and the victim knows this but is powerless against it. Teachers wash their hands of the issue once the restorative process has apparently been accomplished. Instead of being properly punished and educated, the perpetrator might expect to be operating as usual within a day or two of restorative justice having been executed.

Bullies know the system is a joke. Victims know the system is a joke. Bullies know they are always going to win because they are not held to account with honesty. Victims know the bullies are always going to win because they are allowed to present themselves in a favourable light with an alternative version of events. Teachers think they've done the right thing because many of the bullies are apparently, to an adult eye who tries to find balance to keep the peace, and to be fair might try to find the best in people, contrite in the restorative justice meetings. And no doubt many bullies do have their own issues to contend with. But victims, if they find the strength to attend RJ at all, feel more powerless and humiliated than ever knowing for the bully it's all an act. It's a system that fails the victims and enables the bullies, and this, Jenny believes, might be one reason why more and more teenagers, unable to express the truth of their situation, are refusing to go to school. They have no other option if they are going to save themselves.

Epilogue

Many years after he left school, Sam is now a young man with a client-facing job, a steady girlfriend and prospects. He enjoys social time with his friends and feels confident in himself out and about. Sam today is a completely different person to the Sam of school days: now reclaimed, he is confident, charming, kind and quietly outgoing.
Sam is good with people and has a wonderful sense of humour. You can see him grow when he is greeted, acknowledged and treated like a person who matters as much as anyone else, and the more he is accepted and respected for who he is when out and about in the world, the more his self-esteem grows. A complete contrast to the erasure and reduction he suffered at school. None of this is rocket science. It's what we all need for personal growth. Sam is a nice person, but nice people are often the ones who come in for it at school where dominance is the name of the game and the 'populars' are often the polar opposite of nice. Post-school life for Sam has been one of

recovery and increasing happiness and confidence. He doesn't talk about his school days because they are irrelevant to him now.

Sam benefited from both CAMHS and antidepressant medication in the dark days, but eventually he felt that he could move on. After his year on medication he was able to come off it and moderate his mood without it. Given the space to relax, find himself and learn a little about life, he weaned himself off the anti depressants, began to structure his life and started to find meaning in day to day living. Jenny and Mike understood Sam's need for self-agency and accommodated it. They did not push him to do anything because they knew this would have a negative effect on him and be counter-productive - he has always been a person who needs self-agency. Instead, they gently encouraged him to take baby steps into adult life, taking care to reinforce in him a knowledge that nothing in life is the be and end all. There are many chances for a young person to achieve and develop once they have left school. In fact, many teenagers like Sam only start to realise their potential once they have left school and found freedom. The traditional way is not the only way, as Sam had proved. But why is it made so difficult for young people who don't fit the norm? Schools send out the 'be and end all' message because, driven by Ofsted, it suits them in their mission to get their results up and look good. And that's fine for the kids who thrive within that system, or who can at least tolerate it, but for the others it's a disaster because it feeds fear of failure and gives out a wrong message that they will amount to nothing if they don't do well enough according to arbitrary developmental standards. In effect, Sam 'left' school at the beginning of Year 10, but he's still ended up with the qualifications he needs to do what he wants in life by doing education differently.

Jenny hopes that by sharing the story of how Sam found happiness and success in his own way, out of the school system, other parents will find the strength and courage to stand up to schools if the worst happens. Bullying, both insidious and overt, has reached dangerous and epidemic proportions in British schools and it's at the core of much school refusal. But the problem is not recognised by schools. Jenny knows parental understanding of bullying can be limited because many teenagers don't admit to being bullied as they are desperate to fit in, or they fear reprisals. But she urges parents to be vigilant before trying to force their child into school if they don't want to go, because there might be hidden horrors waiting for them there. Most teens can summon the resilience to deal with minor issues within friendship groups or classes, but when minor issues become protracted and serious problems, it's likely time to stop pushing them into school and listen.

Even though it came as a great relief, Jenny and Mike initially felt scared after they had made the decision to walk away from school, because they had absolutely no idea about how the different ways of doing education would play out. There's very little awareness of the alternatives, and, wrongly, the perception is that the only alternative is to go private or to home school. But once Sam had embarked on his new educational path, they, like Sam, felt liberated. Although Sam had wanted to return to his secondary school because he had had good times there to begin with and it was all he had ever known, it became obvious that he could not return; it was far too difficult for him to break through the barriers and restrictions and contend with the many threats to his well being. Jenny has CAMHS to thank for recognising Sam's school phobia, but she also feels Sam should not have had to wait for official confirmation from CAMHS to be able to access alternative provision. It was the push pull effect of trying and failing to get back into school that kept them in a state of hiatus for so long. If school had listened to Sam, read his behaviour intelligently and acted quickly, independently of CAMHS, so much wasted time and pressure could have been avoided. Instead of reading Sam's behaviour as 'failure to attend' it should have been 'needs a different approach because something's wrong', and they should have trusted and respected Sam and his parents. All schools should have the willingness and ability to flex when things aren't working, without resorting to threats, fines or other punishments. Jenny has since found support from one or two of the many online support groups for parents whose teenagers refuse school that have sprung up in the last decade. Her own path was a solitary one because she thought they were the only ones. However, Sam, a private person, would not have considered meet ups or group help sessions even if Jenny had known of any. Only now that Sam is out of the education system can Jenny feel freer to talk about their experiences of school, though Sam prefers to keep his thoughts, feelings and experiences to himself. He says he doesn't care any more; that was then and this is now. He has moved on.

Jenny, however, finds comfort in knowing her family never were the only family in the country who experienced the catastrophe of school refusal; it is, in fact, a hidden epidemic. The truth is, too many young people are being failed by an underfunded, over stretched and often wilfully careless education system that prefers to project a positive image of itself rather than sincerely address the complexities of modern schooling, and there is no comfort in that. The modern school system does not understand anxiety and school phobia, and it refuses to recognise the extent of bullying that goes on.

Suspicious of school refusers because teachers believe they are nice people doing the right thing, the system punishes victims with threats and fines instead of changing practices to help them. For Jenny, it's illogical. Schools do not punish bullies effectively and their victims know it. Very often bullying goes on behind the scenes or is sneaky so teachers might not be aware of what's going on, but the victims of it are hyper aware. Twisting the idea of resilience, the word has become a weaponised catchphrase to place the onus on the victim to have to deal with situations they shouldn't have to, and victims are forced back into situations teachers have no idea about.

Who hasn't heard about the kid on the school bus who routinely has things thrown at her? Who hasn't heard about the young person in the classroom nobody will work with? Who hasn't heard about the teenager who was beaten up by a gang walking home from school? The list of everyday occurrences could go on and on and yet somehow this catalogue of ruined young lives is shrugged off as 'teenage behaviour.'. Jenny believes all this must change before schools can start to function effectively for everyone, starting with proper respect between individuals and proper consequences for bullying. Jenny would never advocate refusing medical intervention when it is necessary: there are of course teenagers who have serious mental health issues not caused by bullying who need the intervention of mental health support and medicine. But these mental health issues, she believes, should not be conflated with school anxiety or school phobia (often caused by bullying), because the issues caused by school will most likely alleviate when the cause is removed, as was the case with Sam. For Jenny, there is no doubt that the school system caused Sam's collapse, and if he had been home schooled, or if there had been an opportunity to do school differently from the outset, his withdrawal from the world would never have happened. She has never been able to point to one single thing that caused Sam's school refusal, she has only been able to collect the clues by looking back. Jenny can only imagine the noise, the onslaught of information and lack of time to process it, the dynamics and, of course, the threat of knives overwhelmed him before he even had time to register what was happening to him. It must have been so scary for him.

Jenny believes Sam did benefit from CAMHS even though he never told the full truth about his situation. They were amazing for him and made sure he got the kind of schooling that would suit him. Unfortunately, however, CAMHS was not able to offer an answer to losing all your friends, loneliness and knives in school. CAMHS is to help young people function in the world, but their focus is on building children's resilience, not on changing societal structures, which is arguably a similarly challenging task and the one that urgently needs to happen. CAMHS has to pick up the pieces of a broken system, and the system will not offer an alternative for young people unless it's recommended by CAMHS. Yet getting to see a CAMHS mental health professional is nearly impossible in some areas of the country, and the young people who have to wait for years are punished with threats of fines under the banner of safeguarding their 'right to an education' because they haven't got a diagnosis. How obviously broken the system is!

Having battled through it, Jenny wants to add her voice to the call for a complete overhaul of how school is done. Flexibility and variety of provision should be at its heart without having to resort to homeschooling or private schools. Clear sanctions for bullying and detrimental behaviour should be given and empathy taught and shown to children from a young age. Pupils should be able to assert their needs without fear of punishment. The huge buildings, long corridors, loud dining halls, lack of control over information being imparted in assemblies, rowdy classrooms and chaotic playgrounds are not suitable for many children. Nor are the startling bells, divisive 'friendship groups', unmonitored toilets, restricted toilet times and uncomfortable, old fashioned uniforms. Add to those structural pressures vaping, drugs, knives and social media, and the pressures for very many young people become unmanageable.

Jenny wants all young people to be able to learn in an environment where they feel safe and happy. And in a world where conformity has a stranglehold over wellbeing, young people also need to learn that we are all different and be able to accept our differences. Schools' efforts to control young people's behaviour increasingly results in worse behaviour, often unseen by teachers, sometimes caused by teachers and sometimes excused by them. For these reasons, Jenny believes schools have become unfit for purpose for many teenagers, and the evidence backs her beliefs. More and more young people are unable to bear the pressures of secondary school so they bow out. More and more parents are finding themselves floundering in a sea of confusion and fear because they do not understand what is happening to their child when they start refusing school. More and more reason, then, to stop and take stock of what we are doing to our young people who are the unhappiest in Europe.

Today, Jenny sits pensively in the front room of her family home where she shed so many tears for her lost teenage son. She is reading the latest online news article about behaviour in schools. The 'behaviour tsar' responsible for the article says schools' 'soft touch' in managing bullying is contributing to the modern teen mental health crisis.

This, she agrees with, marvelling at the infuriating reality that to call out the system with credibility you have to be a 'behaviour tsar' but to call out the system as a mum who has seen her son's life all but destroyed by school, you're an annoyance to be treated with suspicion. And if you are a young person who refuses to participate in the system because you know the odds are stacked against you and you cannot win, you are medicalised as 'anxious' then you and your family are treated as lacking in resilience or defective in some way.

Jenny reflects that in her family's corner of the UK there will be mums, dads and carers waking school-refusing teenagers to try to get them off to school so that they themselves can then get off to work and life can go on, unaware that their child is actually unable to navigate the system and is perhaps facing bullying, but they are impotent to say or do anything about it. They will force their child into school for fear of being judged or fined, or because they genuinely believe they are doing the right thing because they trust school is the best place for children, just like she and Mike had once done. Then, slowly but surely, they will find themselves with a teenage tragedy on their hands. Jenny feels weighed down by this knowledge. This scenario is replicated in up to a million homes across the UK because statistics at the time of writing this narrative indicate there are a million absentees from school on any given day. A reflection of the grim fact that Britain's kids are unhappy at school and they are not coping. Jenny just about managed to hang on to her job, finding ways to cover the turmoil and present a normal face to the world, but she wants all the people who find themselves struggling to understand they can turn their backs on the school system and do education differently once it becomes clear their young person really cannot cope with school, and that the young person they love and care for will feel better when they no longer have to go to school. It can be done, and in so many cases it must be done, to save the young person at stake. There are other ways of doing school out there, some of them even funded by mainstream schools. Jenny remembers the anguish of those terrible, terrible days of sickness, headaches, tummy aches followed by a total shut down, and would be happy if her story provides hope to even one family struggling as they struggled. If she could give parents of school-refusing teenagers out there any single piece of advice it would be to believe things can and will get better, and to stand your ground if school threatens you. There is a lot your teenager will not be able to tell you, so do what's best for them, not what's best for the school. Life is peaceful in Jenny's family household now that the threat of school is forever over, but what happened to Sam was just the start of the epidemic of teenagers who, post pandemic, find they simply cannot do school so refuse because it's all they can do to save themselves. Jenny believes it wasn't the pandemic that caused this en masse school refusal, despite a popular narrative that it was. The pandemic gave parents and young people a glimpse of how school can be done differently for those many, many kids for whom it does not work. It also made it harder for schools to force strugglers back in because they had been told to stay away for so long. Jenny believes something else, too, truly understanding it more and more as she lives alongside the amazing young adult Sam has become. That Sam is not a victim who, unable to fit in, was not able to cope with a properly functioning school system as it should be. No. Sam knew school was wrong for him. He disliked things that the so called 'popular kids' his age got up to, he knew there was no way he could flourish in his school, so he refused to go in to protect himself from any further harm. In doing this he showed courage, determination and self belief. In doing this he showed resilience. He was, and is, brave and remarkable. Jenny still feels ashamed of trying to get Sam into school in those early days of his school refusal, and she winces at the anguish this must have caused him. But she's proud that she stopped and looked - really looked - and read Sam's behaviour before catastrophe struck. Yes, this period of his life was extremely difficult for Sam and for the whole family, but she and Mike had proved to Sam that they were on his side and their family was now stronger for it.

Jenny has made peace with the fact that she will never know everything about Sam's school history. All she could do was understand and help him the best she could. She understood enough to back him when he refused to go in, and now that school is long gone that's all that matters. She can look back and know she did the right thing.

'Thanks Mum,' Sam said to Jenny out of the blue the other day. 'You believed in me and trusted me. I feel like a stronger person now, and I think I'm good at helping other people in trouble because I understand.'

He is right. Understanding is key, and in a way his troubled school days have provided him with a gift because he knows what the powers that be do not. He has been there. He is not anti-school and he is not angry. He knows school was not the right place for him and he is enjoying life now he feels able to explore his own abilities and interests freely and without judgement. But Sam never, ever talks about his school days and when Jenny tries to bring the subject up he is not interested. 'I'm a different person now and it no longer matters', he says firmly, so this book is Jenny's voice, not his.

'Don't worry, Mum, it'll all be fine' is Sam's mantra these days, and with that, Jenny watches him go off to work with a spring in his step and a smile and a wave goodbye.

Jenny has not used the teachers' real names in her story because she wants to trigger enlightenment, not hate.

Tips from what Jenny herself learned:

When things go wrong...

1. Parents can ask schools to try a reduced timetable, which might help some anxious young people if their aim is to return to school.

2. Stand up to the school if they try to fine you when your child is too anxious to attend. Insist they look closely at behaviour and put your young person's safety and wellbeing first.

3. Try to read the behaviour your young person is showing you, especially when they cannot talk. What are they trying to tell you through school refusal that they do not feel able to verbalise?

4. Ask yourself does your young person have an undiagnosed illness?

5. Know that there are other ways of doing school. You can find support groups on social media to help you navigate the various options.

Printed in Great Britain
by Amazon